ANXIETY IN RELATIONSHIP

The Ultimate Guide to Relationship Anxiety; the Symptoms, Causes, and Recovery Methods for Couples.

By Scarlett Jones

circumstances will any legal responsibility or blame be held against the publisher for any reparation, damages, or monetary loss due to the information herein, either directly or indirectly.

Respective authors own all copyrights not held by the publisher.

The information herein is offered for informational purposes solely, and is universal as so. The presentation of the information is without a contract or any type of guarantee assurance. The trademarks that are used are without any consent, and the publication of the trademark is without permission or backing by the trademark owner. All trademarks and brands within this book are for clarifying purposes only and are owned by the owners themselves, not affiliated with this document.

TABLE OF CONTENTS

INTRODUCTION

artner and friend relationships usually provide pleasure and comfort. However, when in relationships, some people may experience persistent anxiety. Doctors call this; relationship anxiety or distress dependent on relationships.

Relationship anxiety encompasses a romantic or friendly relationship with extreme worries. Even if healthcare professionals are aware of this form of anxiety, it is not included in the Diagnostic-and-Statistical Manual of Mental Disorders.

In comparison to other types of anxiety, such as common anxiety disorder or panic, physicians have no clear guidelines for diagnosing or treating anxiety in relationships.

Relational anxiety encompasses other aspects of social anxiety disorder. More precisely, both conditions may cause a person to have severe rejection discomfort.

This book will discuss the symptoms and causes of anxiety and some care and recovery strategies for couples.

CHAPTER 1
RELATIONSHIP ANXIETY AND HOW TO IDENTIFY IT

Every relationship is somewhat schizophrenic. There is a natural tendency to be closer to the person you have some relation with—a desire to come closer by sharing your thoughts, pleasures, dreams, and desires.

However, there is a tendency to want to distance himself from her. The desire for independence, vulnerability avoidance, remains free and unburdened.

Both these inclinations are natural, thus create a healthy twilight and flow when they are done maturing. Which then helps relationships to mature gradually.

This is more like the pairing of skating figures where one moment, hand in hand, man and woman are together and in the next instant are far apart but linked by a shared rhythm. However, they remain connected at the opposite ends of the rink to music guided by the same choreographed routine.

But what would happen if one of the figure skaters could not maintain the rhythm? What if one team member declined to meet the other? But did he refuse to be segregated from the other? They would suffer from their success. Badly, it may be called "Awkward On Ice."

Anxiety can easily spill into our relationships and create the same kind of problem. Some of us are plagued by the fear of being similar to others. These anxieties also centered on feelings of weakness, inadequacy, or the fear of assuming responsibility. The solution to these feelings is very often to find ways to gain emotional distance.

These connections often do not gain momentum. They stumble, lose direction, and ultimately die of a lack of deep respect.

A different kind of anxiety around relationships is the reverse. This insecurity will contribute to one's attachment to others. Your partner, friend, or even your child's freedom can sound frightening.

Such fears often lead one to demand intense attention, affection, and time from a partner. There is a reliance on constant reassurance. The person who receives these requests will quickly be drained. Each attempt to show genuine love and commitment is never enough. It is never enough. Such relationships break up under pressure.

Anxiety has crush-related capabilities. However, even if a relationship survives this stress, you can not depend on it to be as complete and fulfilling as anxiety would be out of the picture.

Bear in mind that the kind of anxiety we concentrate on has a specific connection with concerns to the commitment and emotional intimacy. This differs from social anxiety, panic, phobia, and other anxiety disorders.

Each of these worries can have a significant impact on relations, but none of them is specifically concerned about emotional intimacy. The distinction differentiates how fear is surmounted.

Signs of Relationship Anxiety

You may wonder if relationship anxiety causes trouble in your life. It can be hard to know; after all, everyone is nervous to some degree, so how you can tell if your relationships with family and friends have been affected.

The following questions can clarify if this is a problem:

1. How often do you worry that your partner will leave you for another person?

2. If he or she is out with friends, do you trust your partner?

3. Do you often require the reassurance of the love and devotion of your partner?

4. Should you worry about how your partner is going to respond to a mistake you made?

5. Are there any talks that you avoid with your partner because you're worried he or she'll get angry?

6. Are you still afraid that your partner is unfaithful?

7. Are you someone who got jealous quickly?

8. Do you have to control the time of your partner; did you know in detail where he or she was, and with whom?

9. Do you not depend on your partner?

10. Would you feel uncomfortable if your partner depends on you emotionally?

11. Have several people said you're hard to get to know?

If you replied' yes' to five or more of the questions, it would be nice to exhibit a very honest talk with your partner. Talk frankly about your anxieties. Try to understand how you can influence your relationship in trying to cope with these fears. Then, work as a team to see how changes can be made, how you connect and improve relationships.

In case you want a clearer sense of how anxiety affects your life, you can complete a three-minute' Brief Anxiety Quiz' on the next page.

Combating Relationship Anxiety: Success Story

To combat anxiety, it is significant to know the main ways in which it appears in your life. Once you know how it seems, it is easier to figure out how to get it going.

There are three ways to show anxiety-emotions, attitudes, and thoughts. The emotional aspect is what everyone talks about when they talk about anxiety. It is the concern and fear that will grow inside you when anxiety has begun to take root.

Physical signs, such as increased heart rate, gastrointestinal discomfort, suddenness, fidgetiness, pacing, sleeplessness, etc.

The thoughts or cognitive effects depend on the anxiety target. Such reflections, however, usually focus on the catastrophic impacts of certain events.

These three facets of anxiety coexist. Anxious thoughts produce disturbing feelings that cause you to behave in specific ways. For example, if there has been a severe storm, and your spouse comes home from work two hours late, then you might start wondering if he or she is in an accident. That thought causes fear, which in turn leads you to start fast. The idea, the feeling, and the action link each other.

We are not only bound, but we can also start to influence each other in ways that are not helpful. They are related to each other in a sequence.

An example should illustrate how this works. Picture Brian and Alicia, a young couple. They have been together for almost a year and are happy.

Previously, Brian was concerned that his career was not progressing quickly enough. He wants to marry Alicia and intends to raise his income before proposing it. In this respect, Brian is determined to be the right supplier and feels unsure of his abilities.

This concern grew stronger later, and as a result, Brian became more worried. The idea of "Loser" being graved across his brow is distracting. Yeah, Brian's complicated with himself.

He wants to work longer hours to start his career (although he works 50 hours a week). As a timid man, a retired man, he doesn't tell Alicia. She will simply ask why and then he will have to say to her about his fears about "Loser," and it's very humiliating. Nope, he'll take care of this at the bottom in his way.

Over the next few weeks, Alicia frequently wonders why Brian is so distracted while together. She also starts feeling a little neglected, as he spends a lot of time at work. She says to herself, "Weird."

Alicia has no background to grasp these changes

without knowing why Brian is distracted or working additional hours. She assumes it must be because he no longer finds her attractive or exciting. Alicia begins thinking about the dedication of Brian to his relationship. She would like to talk to Brian about her concerns, but she won't risk being told her suspicions are right. It'd be catastrophic. Then, Alicia wants to dial her own and withdraw emotionally.

Over time, Brian assumes Alicia's being less careful and affectionate, which is a sign that she needs more time for herself. He thinks, "maybe I moved her too hard" and agrees he will respect her distance requirement. He can do this by working more in the office and not disturbing her by demanding too much of her time.

Naturally, Alicia believes that Brian's support in this way confirms his lack of interest (or self-absorption). Her fear and anger are becoming ever more significant.

She starts to inquire if she is supposed to end the relationship before she gets hurt. We can see how this process is increasing and expanding with time.

10

IDENTIFYING RELATIONSHIP ANXIETY

I don't think any human being who is attracted to other people can say that they never felt concerned about a relationship. Still, relationship fear, which is a direct result of your relationship feeling insecure, takes things to another degree. You are worried about all sorts of things that might have a negative effect or ruin your relationship.

In case you've had bad experiences in the past, your brain will have learned to respond in a way and expect trends to happen again.

You could live with constant rates of underlying anxiety about your relationship, or it could cause waves of tiny, seemingly insignificant things. You started doubting yourself and doubt the feelings of your partner towards you.

When you think that your feeling might be anxiety about relationships, the listed telling signs will help you identify whether it is a concern for you.

1. You Believe the End is Near

No matter how well your relationship is doing. You cannot overcome the nagging feeling that you're going to go a little' Titanic' and hit an iceberg before you sink on board.

Even the least significant discrepancy between yourself and your partner has the fear that your odds have well and truly bite the dust.

2. You're Jealous

Jealousy is a pretty universal emotion, but if it gets out of hand, no relationship can survive.

You will not necessarily show signs of jealousy that your partner will change their behavior, and it may well push them away. But if one thing is sure, it will certainly make you miserable.

If you were deceived in the past, it's no wonder that you get jealous, but it would make you nervous.

3. You are Controlling

You control your anxiety, which means that you are desperately controlling your relationship so that you don't get hurt. You feel that if you have a handle on precisely what is happening, then it will be all right.

4. You are too relaxed

Although this may sound counter-intuitive, one way to control things is always to go the extra mile to satisfy your partner and be the person you think they want you to be.

They can somewhat have no good reasons to bail out the relationship in this way. After all, they get what they want every time, so what's to talk about?

5. You're reluctant to commit.

This is all about self-preservation. Although it may not seem so logical, you may be reluctant to lower your protective walls and move towards a more serious relationship, which can be as a result of you being afraid that the relationship would end. You do not want to be exposed to hurt.

Maybe you have been burnt due to your commitment to someone in the past, and this now fosters your anxieties.

6. Questioning Your Compatibility

You ask questions about your relationship with your marriage phobia, and you try to find excuses why you and your partner simply are not compatible.

Most times, you find things so insignificant that they can easily be solved, but that's not how you see them. You see them as mines waiting to be seized.

(Truly, your anxiety may also be focused on real differences which may prove to be too broad to overcome convictions, such as the way you believe about marriage or children, or where you would like to live in the long run.

7. You get angry

You're always on the brink, which makes it easier for you to lose your patience if something happens that causes your agony. It would be quite hard not to burst since you do expect something to go wrong.

But, because you're insecure in your relationship, you probably worry that your explosion will change your feelings.

8. You ask many questions.

You are never glad to accept an explanation. You ask questions and interpret the responses, bringing their words into your head and trying to find a hidden meaning.

9. You do not enjoy sex.

This might be a result of your uncertainty about the relationship that makes relaxing in the bedroom challenging for you. If you are a woman, you fight to achieve sexual satisfaction as frequently (if at all), and if you are a man, you could struggle to make it first.

Your sex drive may diminish because of these bedroom deceptions, and your relationship's intimacy may suffer.

10. Come Across as Cold

Your relationship anxiety may mean that your partner thinks you're cold, stand-off, or remote. You are defensive, and if they enter and then damage you, they don't like to expose any holes in your armor.

11. You are too Clingy

And, on the reverse side, your relationship anxiety

may mean that you go entirely the other way. You may constantly need physical and verbal affections with assurances that you still love yourself and that you have not changed your mind since they were last saying it 5 minutes ago.

Overcoming Your Relationship Anxiety

The relationship is an awful thing to experience. This means you can't appreciate the magic of love, and you are just too worried that your partner will come out of it.

Ironically, your partner might want to put an end to all the negative energy that you worry about in your relationship.

Luckily, you can do a lot to relax your mind and begin to change your outlook for you to enjoy your relationship rather than living in constant stress.

Here are some easy ways to overcome your relationship anxiety:

1. **Always remember that it's all going to be all right.**

In case you are in the middle of a disintegrating relationship, it can quickly feel like the end of the world.

However, it can be challenging to keep things in focus and see the light at the end of the tunnel when all those emotions rush in.

So how do you go about it? It's as easy as to note that whatever happens, it's all alright. Think back and have a rethink. It's very okay if you have had a heartbreak before, and you just got through it.

When you met your friend, you were perfectly fine, and life would go on after them if things ever go south.

Your life won't end if your relationship does, and being in a relationship isn't everything and would not be everything. A friendship can be fantastic, but it never determines you.

If somebody doesn't want to be with you, you can't do anything about it. You deserve to be with someone who moves heaven and earth.

When panic begins to rise, just murmur to yourself that all is all right. If you say it to yourself enough, you will start to believe it sooner or later.

However, the less you fear the end of the relationship, the more you can relax and enjoy it at the moment.

2. Discuss how you feel with your partner

A lack of communication or miscommunications also causes anxiety about relationships, so it's best to talk with your partner proactively.

If you plan to see each other, be the one to look for concrete details, like when and where. And this does not mean that you always have to decide (though you want to share this responsibility), it does mean that you are the organizer in your relationship.

You could say that it's just an extension of being too controlled, but it's not. You haven't driven any small thing by yourself, yet you are talking about flying.

If your relationship is more established but still anxious, talk from a place of honesty and openness to your partner.

Explain how you feel and let them know this isn't about them, but your past experiences. Try to provide examples of situations that are difficult for you and how they can alleviate your fears.

If the relationship is severe, and you are willing to do everything you can to provide you with peace of mind.

This may also assist you in expressing your feelings more pityingly if your anxieties cause you to do something that upsets them. You will know that what you say (or do) not necessarily mean all the time and that it can help you overcome your feelings by not adding fuel to the fire.

So asking your partner about your anxiety will make you feel better. In this regard, you will feel like a weight is lifted off your shoulders, and you will be confident that they don't go anywhere if they react positively and with love.

3. Build your independence

If you're in love, you may feel that you're happy to live in your partner's pocket if you can, but losing yourself in your relationship is sure to boost your anxiety about your relationship.

If you just start defining yourself in terms of your relationship, you put too much pressure on it to be successful in the long term. Who would you be, after all, if you'd break up?

Make sure you do things consciously for yourself and

keep a life apart from your partner. Try to retain the things that make you unique, perhaps because your partner was first drawn to you.

Your companion is not your' other half,' and they are not to complete you. You are fine and complete as you are. It's beautiful to be in a relationship, but not crucial to your happiness.

4. Stop analyzing your every move consciously.

People comment throwaway. You don't ponder on every word you say or evaluate how your nervous mind can view every text message you send. You should, therefore, not allow the little stuff to influence your state of mind.

5. Note that you control your mind, and it doesn't control you.

You're not at your mind's mercy. You have the power to guide, shape, and train it. You may still experience fear once you've realized this, but you can recognize it for what it is and allow it, rather than allow it to consume you and guide your behavior.

Breaking Relationship Anxiety Pattern

Let's see how this kind of pattern can be changed to create more happy and healthy relationships.

We will begin with a short one-issue question: the secret to getting rid of this form of disruptive anxiety is:

1. Take a psychoanalyst five days a week, lay on the couch, and say anything about what comes to your mind.

2. Burning incense, drumming, chanting, eating a strictly vegan diet for six months, and wearing paisley bell

3. A combination of clear communication and remedial experiences.

The response is, get ready......" C. "Clear communication was a gift, right? Definitely. Had it being that Brian or Alisha had been open about what they thought, there is a high possibility that their situation would never have spiraled down.

Then, it is worth noting that some people do not have enough clear communication to save their relationship. It occurs when one or both partners have particularly strong suspicions that they are intimate.

The anxiety is so deeply rooted that there is still uncertainty even with excellent communication. It's like talking to somebody afraid to fly and asking him or her about an outstanding aviation safety record.

The knowledge can be simple, precise, and even scientifically acknowledged. But at a gut level, he knows the plane on which he or she flies surely falls from the sky and crashes.

There is something else essential to help this person conquer the fear of flying.

Corrective Experiences as The Key to Change

Corrective experience is essential to break the worrying patterns we have discussed. A therapeutic experience is one that successfully repels any overwhelming fear. It rectifies a lie, and it cures a distortion. To be corrective, the interpretation must contradict the very basis on which one's anxiety remains alive.

These bases are always based on falsehoods. "Nobody could genuinely love me if they knew the true me." "I think people think I'm a success, but that's only a façade- if they could see the facts, it would show me that I'm an impostor." "If I don't let that person work out in my life and things, I would be utterly devastated." Not by thought, but by practice. It's a dive into the moment that gives it energy.

Let me explain. Let me elaborate. Using the fear of the flight example again, a corrective experience would be a person who got on an airplane and remained calm during the flight (no screaming, no rolling on the island, no hanging on the stewardess like a teddy bear), and landed safely.

The person would have experienced flying in a plane safely and calmly. The lie "If I get on that plane, I will crash and die" has been falsified. Score one step for truth and get rid of the fear of flying.

However, to thoroughly reduce this concern, the corrective experience would have to be repeated in various settings over a while. In this case, the person would have to take other short and long flights with his companions and solo from different airports.

The hope is that the discomfort of several corrective encounters should be fully resolved so that it is no longer an active force in one's life. This is democracy. Yeah….Democracy!.

Success Story: Brian And Alicia Corrective Experiences

Encounters this young couple of corrective contacts would have required a lot of different behavior. Concerning Brian, it would mean talking to Alicia rather than covering her insecurities. It would also mean he did not try to work more hours simply to avoid his insufficiency (this means he had worked diligently throughout his career).

Alicia's therapeutic interactions will mean talking about her anxiety that Brian is no longer committed to the relationship, rather than avoiding talks. When her apprehension continued even after she was convinced, she would have to remain fully committed and attentive to the relationship. This is directly opposite to the reaction she had to avoid involvement.

When Alicia and Brian continued to act in ways that

were counter to their fears, their fear would gradually decrease. With time, both of them could break the stranglehold of relation anxiety with repeated corrective experiences. We would, therefore, find a sense of liberation and emotional communication we had never experienced before.

Using this Information

The trick to using the story of Brian and Alicia is to make an honest evaluation of your worries, anxiety, and reactions to establishing close and intimate relations. Write these down and then consider how plausible each of these concerns is, in your present relationship.

At this point, it may be helpful to have a friend or advisor to review the list and give your opinion on the relevance of these products.

Then pick those concerns that are unfounded and seem to be significant obstacles to the creation of a more fulfilling partnership. Take time to think about the corrective experience as an excellent first step to overcome this fear?

The panic that part not, just take your time. Take your time. Come up and be as specific as possible with several things you can do. Then pick one and go on to bring the experience into your life. Just as in the above example, Brian had to talk to Alicia about his insecurity and his ability to provide. He would then have had to stop spending more time at work.

This is the kind of realistic and "real world" insight to provide a solution. Don't settle for anything less. Initially, corrective experiences create anxiety, and this is one of the reasons they're' corrective' because you face something you're afraid of. If your behavior doesn't cause you to be nervous, it is possibly not very closely related to your anxieties.

In that case, you are unlikely to be very helpful. Do something that demands a degree of bravery. Then you'll know you're on the right path.

CHAPTER 2

HOW TO LIVE WITH PARTNER WITH RELATIONSHIP ANXIETY

Being in a relationship with someone having problems with anxiety disorder can be stressful. Sometimes it can sound like fear, but someone who wobbles between you and your friend is a third person in the relationship because this person always sows doubts and uncertainty.

Nobody has prepared you for it, and you cannot choose for whom you fall for. There is no high school dating class, much less meeting someone who is mentally ill.

Nonetheless, there is no need for anxiety to ruin the relationship or to make it difficult to enjoy. However, you can love each other more deeply by understanding fear in general and how it affects both your partner and your relationship. Education can also relieve a great deal of stress.

These books break down all you need to learn and do when someone is anxious to talk about: how to help your partner, how anxiety can impact your relationship, searching for your mental health, and more. Keep reading if you want to ensure that your partnership does not become a third person.

Anxiety-Filled Conversation

If you ask or deduce it after monthly meetings, there will be a point when your partner discloses that they have to deal with fear. It is a critical time in the relationship, therefore be sensitive and do not judge. Thank them for trusting you with this knowledge, which they probably did not share with many people.

Understanding Anxiety and Knowing What It is Doing to Your Partner

Learning fear and what your partner is doing will help you to understand and assist the partner with some basic facts about anxiety. Psychologist Dave Carbonell, Ph.D. psychiatrist Dr. Helen Odessky, among others, suggested bearing these in mind:

- Anxiety is normal, and it's present in everybody. It becomes a problem or disorder only if it is severe.

- Anxiety is a real problem, not a composite. It's a problem in mental health.

- Anxiety can be a crippling condition that prevents people from working and living a healthy life.

- Anxiety causes people to experience flight and battle responses and worry about life-threatening issues, which include whether a partner may cheat or leave.

- You can't "cure" or "fix." Anxiety

- Many people who have anxiety disorder wish they never had it. They are concerned that their anxiety is a burden for others.

- There are millions of people who have great relationships and are happy despite dealing with anxiety.

- Symptoms of anxiety, either consistently or not, may occur in waves, which means people with anxiety disorders or problems can have periods when they have no symptoms.

- Anxiety is not rational or logical. It causes people to worry about something, although there is no evidence that it is worth worrying. It also causes them to act irrationally sometimes. Your partner probably knows that.

- Anxiety is not a weakness.

- Anxiety can be treated; psychotherapy can alleviate symptoms and teach people how to manage them better.

How Anxiety May Affect Your Relationship

When dealing with someone nervous, your partner probably spends a lot of time worrying and ruminating about everything that may go wrong or already went wrong. Listed below are some examples of thoughts and questions in such brain:

- What if he doesn't love me as much as I love him?

- What if he's hiding something from me?

- What if she is lying to me?

- What if he lies to me?

- What if he's going to cheat me?

- What if she likes someone else better?

- What if we break up?

- What if he ghosts on me?

- What if he doesn't reply to my messages?

- What if anxiety ruins our relationship?

- What if I am only the first to reach out?

Most people have some of these worrying thoughts; at least, they are a normal part of a relationship, particularly a new one.

However, people with anxiety problems or an anxiety disorder tend to have this anxiety more frequently and more intensely.

"Our thoughts are taking over and heading straight into the worst-case scenario," said MicheleneWasil, a therapist who understands both personal and psychiatric anxiety.

Anxiety causes physiological effects, including shortness of breath, sleeplessness, and anxiety. Anxious people can react to stress with the fight or flight response as if stress were a physical attack.

Sometimes, distressing thoughts motivate your partner to act in ways that stress the relationship. For example, psychologist Jennifer B. Rhodes said, people with anxiety often check their partner's involvement with unsecure approaches. These strategies usually address one of their anxious convictions.

Let us say that your partner is anxious to be the first to initiate communication. You don't like him as much as he wants you to, so he begins to worry because you do not send the first text as often as he does. Anxiety intensifies, and he starts to think that if he did not reach out first, you could never talk with him.

He agrees that it's a brilliant idea to fantasize about you for a while to cure this fear. This forces you to communicate first. Perhaps a couple of times, you'll touch him before he feels good, knowing you'd make an effort. The proof encourages him to doubt his unreasonable and nervous conviction that you will not hit first. Though, it's not the right approach.

Unfortunately, there are many behaviors in relationships motivated by anxiety. Here are a few more examples:

- Being controlling

- Perfectionism

- Passive-aggressive behavior or being avoidant

- Being overly critical

- Being irritable and angry

- Having difficulty focusing and being distracted. In a situation that you are in a relationship with someone with a social anxiety issue, the anxiety is likely to affect your social life, thereby preventing or exhibiting offensive behavior

- Perfectionism

When you meet somebody with social anxiety, you may not be able to bring your partner to all the social events or meetings you want to attend. Like other types of anxiety, this may give rise to disagreements or cause you two to grow apart.

How to Deal With It

Anxiety doesn't have to jeopardize your relationship. You can have a healthy relationship through the right coping strategies and avoid anxiety from creating too much tension.

Always encourage your friend or partner to meet with a therapist. When you look after someone, you are tempted to support them by trying to act as a surgeon. The problem is that you are not a therapist, and it will be emotionally draining to try to play that part. It could even make your partner resent you.

You are not liable for your partner's counseling, and this is why the partner should be carefully directed to meet with a therapist. A therapist can help them improve their treatment of anxiety in and out of a relationship.

If you have a serious, long-term relationship, seek therapy for couples. Some of the problems of anxiety can depend on your relationship.

Meeting with a couple of counselors will relieve your partner from the strain. Instead of pushing them to do something for themselves, you encourage them to take part in counseling.

If your partner accepts or resists your suggestion to go to treatment, you should do it yourself. This helps you develop the skills needed to understand and deal with the anxiety of your partner. Your health provider can also teach you how to support your anxious partner more effectively.

It's very easy to forget to take care of yourself if you meet someone with anxiety. You can always reflect on your mental health by going to therapy.

Learning How to Communicate Better About Anxiety

Anxiety can be frightening; therefore, you should make sure you don't think about it. However, one of the most effective ways to deal with anxiety in a relationship is to talk to your partner openly, honestly, and directly about it.

"It is crucial to have candid talks together about what they feel and to validate those feelings," says therapist Daryl Cioffi.

You need to encourage your partner to open up to

show their anxiety. Try to listen, stand up for yourself, or take your fear personally.

Managing Your Reaction to Relationship Anxiety

It is easy to take it seriously and get angry when your partner talks about his or her fears in your relationship. "Anxiety can be easily understood as egoism, denial, or a desire to separate itself," said therapist Michael Hilgers.

"You're going to want them to get over it," said Hilgers. "You'd like them not to think about it."

You can turn this ineffective default response into something more positive by practicing your coping skills. Here is an example to help you practice: assume your partner is afraid that she will betray you; when you take this seriously, you might think she has this insecurity because she hates you or because she thinks you're the kind who would cheat.

As soon as you do it, you can begin to feel frustrated. You might respond defensively and say something meaningful.

"You will only worsen the problem if you can't bend without bullying," said Hilgers.

Then you're going to strike again. Skip forward one hour later, and you fight. The point is bubbling. Perhaps you don't even know why you fight.

Instead of making the tension rush up, take a moment to relax. Note that most likely, the fear isn't about you, and you're not the source; it's your partner.

Ask respectfully to what your partner feels. Something like, "I'm so sorry you feel like this. That must be tough. Can we do anything to help you feel more confident about that?"

It's more important to manage your reactions than to manage your partner," said Talkspace therapist Marci Payne. It can help you to be there and set boundaries for your partner. If the fear of your partner causes you to freak out every time you bring it up, it will not help you.

Setting Boundaries

You need to find a compromise between being compassionate and setting boundaries when you meet someone with anxiety. Once you realize how their anxiety affects their behavior, you can slow them down for behavior, which you usually may not have patience.

Nonetheless, this should be minimal. Even severe mental disorders do not allow people to be cruel or hurtful.

"Not always be the bender," said Hilgers. "If you always give way to the fear of your partner, you will become resentful and angry, not to the anxiety, but your partner."

You should tell your partner that these behaviors, including during anxiety and stressful periods that cause intense anxiety:

- Threats

- Insults

- Accusations

Endeavor to let your partner know that they are going to take steps to improve their anxiety. This is another part of setting limits.

Shifting Your Mental State to Relieve Stress

Anxiety brings about stress, and we naturally take this as an issue, nothing else. This is brought about by fear and anger.

Dr. Carol Kershaw, a clinical psychologist, recommended that couples should try to change their mindsets on anxiety. We should develop curiosity about it instead of just seeing it as a source of stress. Trying to understand the fear makes it harder to get angry.

"Curiosity will turn away anxiety and worry," said Kershaw. "You cannot experience two at once."

Supporting Your Partner With Relationship Anxiety Issue

The distinction between helping your spouse and becoming the unpaid non-official therapist of your partner. A therapist won't hold your partner while he or she cries or takes them out to alleviate anxiety.

The researcher Janet Ruth Heller, Ph.D., spent many years with her husband, who has issues about anxiety. When his fear flashes, she reminds him calmly of what is going on. She also takes him to walks, dinner, or a film.

"These things make him feel safe and loved, which reduces his anxiety," she said.

Her story shows that a caring and long-term relationship can be formed when someone is dating with care.

Listed below are other ways you can help your partner:

Always acknowledge their progress on Anxiety Problems.

Once your partner takes measures to work on fear, try to notice it. Alicia Raimundo, a speaker, mental health advocate, and anxious person, suggested partners "celebrate their strength" when possible.

Listen always!

Even if you're tired or feel like your partner is saying something, try to listen carefully. It allows them to learn that you care about it.

Do you have any rituals or hobbies you use to take care of your mental health? Do you have a partner? Perhaps you are meditating, exercising, or hearing soothing music. If that is the case, consider including your friend.

"With boyfriends, I have done breathing exercises, and it's very personal," Nina Rubin, a life trainer, said. "We have sat across and breathed with the same slow pace."

Including your partner into rituals like these can help you both reduce your anxiety.

What Not to Do

To avoid aggravating the anxiety, creating more stress ad hurting your partner, do not:

- Dismiss their anxiety

- Criticize them for having this anxiety

- Allow maladaptive anxious habits by indulging them too much

- Take everything up yourself

- Try to be their therapist

- Try fixing your partner

- Recommend drugs for their anxiety issues

- Lose your temper or patience when it gets worse

Anxiety can affect your relationship and serves as an opportunity to deepen your partner's understanding and love. The convictions behind their fear are part of who they are.

You can, however, support your partner by learning about anxiety or seeking help from a mental health professional to improve your mental health. Your friendship can then become more profound and more joyful.

HOW ANXIETY CAN AFFECT YOUR RELATIONSHIP

The generalized anxiety disorder (GAD) can harm several aspects of your life, including your relationships.

These are two specific ways in which your distress can lead to problems in maintaining relationships with others, and techniques can be implemented (under the guidance of a specialist in mental health) to help you manage their unhealthy attachments.

Being Dependent

Many people with GAD hold their partners (or friends) closely and are continually relying on them for support and reassurance.

In addition to being overly dependent, people with GAD can feel inclined to overthinking and prepare for all worse circumstances. They are unable to reject and try constant communication (and be nervous if a partner or friend fails to respond quickly).

People with GAD and overly dependent relationships can also be angry with the people they feel to be dependent on, ac.

Fighting Problem-based Dependency

When you develop overly dependent relationships, find ways to cope, and rely more on yourself to feel better because your partner or friend can be put under pressure.

For example, if you are angry or suspicious about these relationships, you should first note that your anxiety can fuel this. However, take some time to think about any hard data (facts), which will help your interest in trying to gain insight.

A therapist specializing in a type of talk therapy called cognitive-behavioral therapy can help you formulate strategies on how to reassure yourself and act on their own rather than needing the comfort of your partner whenever you are anxious.

Being Avoidant

Some people with GAD become avoidant of relationships as a means of dealing with their anxieties on the other hand. They can avoid negative emotions (e.g., deception or frustration) because they do not reveal their feelings, open them up, or are vulnerable. Anyone avoiding close relationships may feel cold, emotionally unavailable, lack empathy, or even stand-off, although they may wish for intimate contact.

Combating Avoidance

Cognitive-behavioral therapy can be useful if you consider yourself too far from other types of treatment, such as psychodynamic psychotherapy. A mental health professional can help someone explore past and present connections with emotions.

Treating Your Anxiety and Relationship Problems

A therapist will also explore the impact of GAD on your relationships. Exploring the feelings more closely, for example, can be a good strategy for someone who tends to avoid relationships. On the reverse side, this strategy can backfire on people who are more emotionally reactive and more reliant on others.

However, it is so imperative to note that medication is often also a critical part of GAD care. While the anxiety medications, such as selective serotonin reuptake inhibitors or serotonin-norepinephrine reuptake inhibitors, are not curative and can help you reduce symptoms to help you feel better as you work with your treatment.

While anxiety can be healthy (it can motivate people and aid them to sense danger within their environment), it is overwhelming and debilitating for GAD people, which can be very harmful to relationships.

But be sure that you can develop healthy, long-term, and fulfilling relationships with others with proper treatment.

CHAPTER 3
ROMANTIC RELATIONSHIP ANXIETY

Sometimes it feels like a dangerous game to pursue a romance. Dating requires a degree of vulnerability and is likely to be hurting or frustrating. Thanks to the unpredictable outcome, people can be quite nervous about their current romantic relationship or the barriers to pursuing a new one.

Many find that untreated anxiety can affect their romantic lives. Individuals with a social anxiety disorder will constantly worry about how others are judging, so they can avoid intimate interactions or dating in general, because of their fear of embarrassment. Others with a common anxiety disorder may have issues with dating or maintaining relationships because they tend to be worried about the loss of their partner. However, it is important to keep in mind that you do not need a diagnosed anxiety disorder to interfere with your romantic relationship. Everyone is vulnerable to daily stress, which is a matter of concern, fear of a partnership, or difficulty interacting with a partner.

Anxiety Checklist

In case you are not sure whether there is anxiety in your romantic relationship, consider moments or issues that worry you. If you are uncertain whether there is anxiety in your romantic life, that causes problems, ask yourself the following questions.

- Do you have those concerns that prevent you from entering into relationships or dating?

- Are you more anxious about sexual intimacy?

- Would you trust your partner deeply to comfort you or ease your anxious thoughts?

- Are you not talking to your partner seriously because you are afraid of conflict?

- Are you constantly afraid your partner will abandon you?

- Are you concerned while your partner is away?

- Would you allow your partner to be unfaithful without proof?

Steps To Manage Relationship Anxiety

-       ***Request help:*** Never think you have to learn how to manage anxiety by yourself in relationships. Consider how individual counseling can help you overcome relationship worries or take steps to make your life happier. Couple advice can also enable people to improve communication and develop problem-solving skills in their relationship.

-       ***Create your desires:*** If you focus entirely on a romantic relationship, you are possibly nervous. Individuals having strong relationships with family and friends and focused attention on their personal goals and interests are likely to become better partners. They are less likely to experience separation or relationship uncertainty.

-       ***Assess your thinking:*** Anxiety makes it difficult to assess objectively whether a concern is legitimate. For example, if you are usually more nervous, you can be persuaded that your partner cheats or plans to leave you when having no existing evidence. Deliberate on whether you need to control your anxiety by healthy habits, better connect with your partner, or answer concerns about your relationship.

- ***Share the beliefs:*** People in relationships often concentrate so much on having someone like them such that they fail to talk for their interests and needs. Compromise is part of any relationship, but it doesn't mean that if something is important to you, you shouldn't express your thoughts or be solid. The sooner you can set a precedent for expressing your desires with one another, the less resentful you are.

- ***Don't run away:*** People who feel insecure in a relationship may be inclined to escape or remove themselves from stuff that causes problems. Avoidance is just a temporary solution and often ends in hot confrontation. Set a standard for resolving issues, even if it feels uncomfortable at first. If you need a third party to promote better communication, do not hesitate to work with or individually with a counselor.

In case you're not sure of where to start, think about your romantic relationship that you worry about the most. How can you deal with this issue in your best version? You may already have an idea of how to improve the relationship and how to handle your anxiety. Yet, support is always available if you don't. Consider who you can recruit to help you handle your anxiety today.

SUCCESS STORY: HOW COPING MECHANISM CAN HELP YOU LOVE AGAIN

A mental health advocate shares her heartbreak story, hard work, and recovery. Before diving into my life story with a mental illness, I want to tell you something first. If you read this, you probably also live with mental illness ebb and flow. In the rough days, desperate nights, and unique challenges, you may have a front line seat. And if you are like me, you might feel guilty that you always suffer, fight, or try to improve your mental health.

I share my story because I was there, and I want to help. I really want to help. I hope that what I have learned from my mental health and the work I have done to get through it can help you.

You must know you are worthy of love. You also deserve a kind and compassionate partner who loves you through the hardest days of your life. You are worthy of a love that embraces your struggles with compassion and gentle understanding. You don't have a responsibility because you have problems that go far beyond your control. I know that thoughts can be loud, and pain can be intense, but you're still deserving at the beginning of each morning, the end of each night, and in every moment in-between.

How It Started

The summer before my college year, I started to experience hot flashes and sporadic bouts of swelling. I felt out of control at that point, and I was told that I had a heart attack or signs of severe physical illness. The more it happened, the more I became scared that it would happen again. I've always been in a nervous state of anticipation. I was reluctant to see a therapist, and in the long run, I was diagnosed with a Generalized Anxiety Disorder (GAD) with my Mom's encouragement. Until that time, I had little knowledge of mental health and no idea what life was like for someone who lived with it. My "usual" revolved around university life. I concentrated entirely on the outside. Before that day, at the end of the summer, I never reflected on myself; I never considered how I felt. My diagnosis marked the start of another realm of life for me. It was as if I was shaken awake— I think my entire mind was stuffed for many years.

Because of the extent of my symptoms, I could not return to school in the fall, initial summer, or subsequent term. My GAD developed into an agoraphobia panic disorder. Sadly, I was physically crippled, and for months I couldn't leave my home alone.

It was a terrible time. I had a continuous state of fear and uncomfortable living, totally isolated from the outside world. It was surprising how quickly my life changed overnight. Somehow, I turned from a wealthy college student with a bright future to a housewife in my head. The agoraphobia was fueled by a concern that there would be another public panic attack. And, I wasn't ready to answer anyone bombarding me with questions from the school.

My new standard has been weekly counseling, constant visits and tests by doctors, regular mental health awareness, and an obsession with bettering. Suddenly, my whole life was to save it.

In this difficult time, I kept dating my college husband: Depression and heartbreak. We had a regular and enjoyable friendship before my diagnosis–I thought of him as my best friend. However, my diagnosis took us both by surprise. Our unconcerned college romance suddenly went wrong with a real crisis in life.

We tried to do a long-distance, but it was hard to adjust. One day, we walk happily through life together, the next day tore apart by a challenge which seemed at the time incomprehensible. He stared helplessly at me, trying to fight for a life that had no pulse anymore. It felt as if I had lost everything except him— I leaned even deeper into this passion. I kept on it like a haven in the storm's eye.

My worst fear came to light eight months after my recovery when our relationship ended. I can't talk about his acts, but I'm sure it wasn't easy or fun to deal with my situation. I experienced crushing pain that I didn't know was possible after our breakup. My mental health continued to fall even faster than before. What was already heavier became heavier, and my pain widened to depression and worsening anxiety. Losing him meant losing a former life's last sliver. There was no escape.

Entering A New Relationship

It had been a year since I started dating Andrew. There have been no reference points or goals since I started working with someone new, but I felt confident that I would take that step forward after a year of focusing on myself. This time I knew that it wasn't going to be perfect, and sometimes I would have to remember who I used to be and who I was, but I did it — we did it.

In my recovery, I was far enough, but still in an active healing place. I had just come out at the other end of the most stressful season of my life, and it was my main priority to preserve my mental health. As a proud promoter of mental health, I shamelessly told Andrew that I was healing. I filled it with all the delicate parts of my life and explained my daily work and self-care to take care of myself.

It had to be fully understood that my safety came first. These admissions came with fear, of course. After all, I wasn't an abandonment outsider. How could I not worry that my problems might be too much for someone else, even if I did have a year of finding out how to handle them?

Yet Andrew didn't bat an eye. A weight lifted off my shoulders— Finally, I got to understand what real acceptance feels like. It only had to be by the right person at the right time. Andrew's level of kindness and desire to learn about my mental wellbeing made it so easy for me to let him in. However, we fell in love quickly and organically. Maybe, it was because I had a love to give that was designed from the ground up.

Seeing the Struggle

I have taught Andrew how to be there for me over the years. The basic difference in this relationship is that I know my mental health now, and I am qualified to advocate for myself when I am struggling. I discovered in counseling that it was all right to ask Andrew for what I wanted in difficult times and encourage him to be that for me. I learned that it was all right to be vulnerable. However, we've learned what has worked and what has not worked. We tried to find the right rhythm for ourselves. We worked hard to connect and discovered a language of love that satisfied our needs.

Only when we moved in with each other could he see the hard edges of mental illness up close. We spent the first four years of our relationship apart, so we could not see all the dark corners of my mental illness. Call it timing, call it a milestone kick, call it to work stress, but my mental health began to collapse after we went in together. I have been dealing with moderate obsessive-compulsive disorder OCD, my entire life, but it worsened beyond measure by the end of 2017. By May 2018, the OCD suffocated me to the point of collapsing. Andrew found himself unexpectedly sharing a table with the mental illness unforgiving, confusing, and terrifying side.

I struggled with Moral Scrupulosity OCD, the constant concern that I was immoral, harsh, offensive, or uncomfortable. These obsessions may lead to repeated mental rituals/loops, finding constant reassurance, and excuses. Sometimes I would find myself frozen, such that I had to repeat a thought in my head until it "felt right." It consumed me totally, and I once again struggled for my life in the way I had never before. Yet I thought about what I was doing instead of being quiet. I welcomed Andrew's help when he worked out how to give it. While it was out of his wheelhouse, he did his best to guide me through something that only my verbal account could understand. And he asked questions, offered help, he listened, and he never stopped giving me the hope that I can go through it and maybe eventually get out of it. In short, my life was saved by communication.

Thinking about the pain saved my life. It saved my life to encourage anyone to be there for me.

Managing Mental Health and Love: A Loud BrainButa Louder Heart

While I was on holiday in Colorado, he proposed to me in September 2018 in the middle of my recovery from my OCD; I can't believe it. I had been battling my mind every day, questioning my worth, succumbing to hours of emotional routines, and struggling for my own life, until then (even moments before!).

I had woken up early in the morning to do my OCD homework. I was on holiday, but he did not stop rehabilitation. How crazy is it to share the space on the same day with these two very different energies, love, and challenge? I couldn't believe I got my most beautiful message in the thick of my struggles; I am still worthy of love. Although I have a brain that likes to persuade me, it was loud and clear at that moment; love always wins.

It was overwhelming for me at first. In addition to my current challenges, it triggered new anxieties instantly because it was new territory for me, after all. But I did the inner work to navigate it with any struggle I went through.

I sat with that anxiety, exhaled it into happiness, and after a few weeks, I was able to feel disconnected. I have learned to turn to written or spoken words during periods of anxiety and fear. Whether I compose or I talk about my pain. Whether it's Andrew, the Instagram group, or my therapist, it always helps me to call for the company to feel alone in my head. The writing was the most beautiful way I could do it.

Every day I'm doing my best, feeling my heart, working, and knowing that I have a loud head, but a louder heart. I'm fortunate to have the best friend who never does the job for me, but with me. Next to me, yea…rightnext to me. A partner who helps me to see fear not as a mountain that blocks the sun but as a mountain to climb. Here is love, here is mental health, here we are all worthy of both!

CHAPTER 4

HOW ANXIETY IS BREAKINGOUR RELATIONSHIPS NOWADAYS

Intimate Relations are mirrors that reflect the best and the worst of us all. They can inflame or soothe our hardships, and they can feel like magic when they're right. Even if they are right, fear will steal the magic and loosen the bond between two people. Both relationships need trust, tenderness, patience, and vulnerability. People with anxiety often have them by lorry and generously give them in their relationship. The problem is that fear can sometimes erode them just as easily.

If you are someone who deals with insecurity, many things make it easy to love you. Each relationship often struggles, and when uncertainty is at stake, the struggles can be quite specific–quite natural and precise.

Anxiety can work curiously, and different relationships are influenced differently so that not all of these are relevant to each relationship. Here are some ways to improve and secure the relationship against the effects of anxiety:

1. Upgrade the emotional resources

You are probably super sensitive to the needs of others and give your relationship openly and abundantly. However, fear can drain these resources as quickly as you invest in the relationship. This is all right–there is plenty of stuff to do with, but it can mean that you have to make sure certain tools are updated. Heap attention, gratitude, affection, touch a lot of touches, and conversation with your partner every time you can.

2. Let your partner always see you as help.

Your partner may be reluctant to' burden' you with concerns, especially if those concerns do not seem as great as those with which you are confronted. People with anxiety have so much energy–without them, it is impossible to live with anxiety–just make sure that your partner knows how big or small their challenges are, sometimes you can also support. Partners of anxious people may tend to dismiss their worries, but this could mean they will not be able to feel nourished and encouraged by you, and that would be a huge loss for you both. Sometimes you need to be careful to be the rock too. Tell, hold, touch, hold, and touch. Nothing cures more than the embrace of the person you love.

3. Let your partner talk about what you think.

While anxious thoughts are highly personal, encourage your partner to do so. It's a key element of intimacy. You also worry about what you have to do, to feel safe, what feels bad for you, and what might go wrong. You will also be able to think of other people (worried people), but be sure you encourage yourself to join in the thoughts that arrest you. Keeping things too much for yourself will increase the gap between two people.

4. It's okay to ask for reassurance–but not too much.

Anxiety has a way to get into it all. If left unchecked, you can doubt what is not worth doubting–like your relationship. To ask your partner for reassurance is all right and very natural. Though, too much and neediness could be felt. Need is the enemy of desire, and the flame will smother over time. Make sure that your partner loves you naturally, without being told because it's wonderful and even better for you.

5. Be vulnerable

Anxiety can have different effects on relationships. In some cases, continuous reassurance may be required. In others, it can cause them to restrain themselves and reduce their vulnerability to heart disease. Vulnerability, open to others, is lovely, and it's a key to successful and healthy relationships. The problem with shielding yourself too much is that it can allow you to deny yourself. Part of intimacy is that you let someone beclose to you than to the rest of the world. This person trusts in the fragile, messy, and untamed parts of you; parts often beautiful, often unbelievable, will always be all right with the person who loves you. You can understand why someone should have open access to these parts of you, but see those fears for what you are and trust that whatever happens if you open up to love and be loved, you will be perfect because you're going to be.

6. **Be careful to project fear into your relationship.**

Nothing, in particular, will cause fear; that's one of the terrible things, and it will look for a target, an anchor to keep it still and make sense. If you are in a close relationship, the bulls-eye sits there and draws your fear to its gravitational pull. This can generate suspicions, envy, distrust, and insecurity. Anxiety can be such a criminal. It doesn't mean your relationship is worth your concern–most definitely not, but your relationship is important, meaningful, and frequently in your thoughts, making it a pretty easy target. Note that it doesn't mean that there is anything to think about just because you are concerned about it. Worry, but then see what it is–fear, not reality. You're loved, and you're anxious, and you're all right. Let this be the truth you hold.

7. **The analysis ends in paralysis.**

There is a saying that "thought leads to insanity" because it does. Is that love? And desire? Or am I kidding myself? What if my heart breaks into tiny jagged parts? What would he do if we didn't like the same music/books/food/films? What if we make reservations and the airline goes on strike? Even if we get sick, what if we both get sick? What if we cannot get a reimbursement and pay the hypothetically? What if he makes me sick?Yeah. I know how it sounds; I hope you know. How you concentrate on it is what's important. So if you focus on the possible problems, they consume the attention until they are large enough to cause their problems. They can drain your strength, enjoyment, and ability to move. You probably know this already, but what to do? Set a period in which you can behave as if things are going to be fine. For instance, worry 10-3 every day and then relax, let go and act as if it was okay. You don't have to believe it – "act as if" only. Tomorrow you will have another chance to think if you need to. Be driven by the evidence, not the worries at 2 a.m.

8. Come closer.

When you focus on every aspect, things get wobbly. You concentrate on things that don't suit your partner or relationship and seek confirmation that your partner is dedicated and loves you at the same time. This may cause you to put your partner off, then pull him or her nearer (Tell me you love me, don't you love me?'). Talk to your partner and, if it is a familiar process, establish a safe way for your partner to indicate when it happens. Agree on what's going to look like. When it happens, make sure that you do not perceive it as a criticism; it does not. It is your partner who asks for consistency in the way you love one another.

9. Hard talks can bring you closer.

Both relationships now and then have to deal with tough things, but fear can make things more dangerous and more complex than they are. The temptation might be to avoid talking to your partner about difficult problems because of worries about what it could do with the relationship. Difficult problems don't walk away–once they hit a boiling point, they fester. Trust that you and your partner will face a tough debate. Relations are based on trust, and it is important to trust that your relationship can be improved through difficult conversations.

10. Let your partner know what you are like

We human beings are complex creatures, and having someone closer to you and your story–even if someone has been with you for quite some time, is the lifeblood of intimacy. People are changing, the stories are changing, and it is even easy to lose contact with the person who you sleeps next tonight. Let your partner know what you're thinking about. Discuss how your feelings, anxiety, job, friendship, partner, and love are influencing you, and how grateful you are for their support.

11. Let your partner know what sets you on fire.

Is there a specific situation that lightens your anxiety? Crowds? Strangers? Entry difficulties? Loud in-car music? To be late? Speak to your partner so that he/she knows what's happening to you if you find yourself in a situation without warning.

12. Be diligent. Be polite. The quick solution is not always the strongest.

As a means to feel better and ease your anxiety, you may be tempted to try to solve a problem or problems quickly. You may feel frustrated with the desire of your partner to wait for a course of action or resist talking about it again, while at the same time being open to your partner's viewing things differently and sometimes clearer. Breathing, communicating, and not thinking the partner takes time or draws out of the discussion due to lack of commitment or because the question is inadequate.

13. Make sure you take care of yourself.

To be in love is crazy, but not taking care of yourself can take your special person away from you. We all tend to do that, but it can be particularly problematic for people with anxiety because once you've got out of control, the rip will bring other things up. It is so important to take good care of yourself. Well, eat (a healthy diet rich in omega 3, low in processed carbohydrates and sugar). Also, regular exercise and meditation will help your brain develop fear. If you feel self-sufficient, think about it like this: it's not fair to expect that your partner will support you through anxiety if all you can do to support yourself is not done. Consider self-care as an investment in you, your relation, and your family. Do note that anything good for you is good for everyone, so talk together with your partner to pursue a healthy lifestyle, including cooking, working out, and meditating.!

14. Understand that your partner will need boundaries

The border that your partner builds can be great to maintain a close, healthy, and connected relationship. Understand that boundaries are not the way of your partner to lock you out, but as a way to protect yourself from' catching up' your anxiety. Maybe you are stressed and need to speak over and over about it, but it doesn't necessarily make yourself, your partner, or your relationship happier. Your spouse can love you and draw a strong emphasis from the last time you talk about something to the next time. Talking is good, but it can drain and cause a problem if you talk about the same thing over and over. You know that your partner loves you, and it is necessary to nurture love and to develop relationships and not to oppose them. Communicate with your partner about what he or she needs to feel all right in the face of your anxiety—giving the limits, helping to keep the relationship strong, caring, and making your lover feel as if he or she can maintain a sense of himself without being overwhelmed by your concerns. Anxiety is infectious, so if your partner (eventually) wants to pull the barrier between your anxiety, let it happen because it will help maintain your relationship's emotional resources, and that will help you both.

15. Smile together

It's so important! Laughter is a natural antidote to anxiety's stress and tension. Laughing together will tighten your connection, and when a stressful couple of days (weeks? months?) has taken place, it will help you both to recall why you have fallen in love. Anxiety has a way to make you forget that life has not always been taken seriously. If your partner has seen the type of your face when you laugh for too long (which would be beautiful and probably one of the reasons he or she fell for you in the beginning), for a reason; a funny video, memories, YouTube, or something.

To fall in love is supposed to be beautiful, but to get close to someone is not the best thing to do without being high and low. Intimacy is a conduit for any possible emotion from the happiness that someone pretty wondrous is as attracted by you as you are to them, to the pain of self-dodge and possible loss, to the comfort, riches, and sometimes peace of a deeper love. Anxiety affects relationships, but you can protect your relationship and make it solid, stronger, and more robust, by being open to its effect and actively reacting to it.

CHAPTER 5

MISTAKES LOVERS MADE WHEN THEY EXPERIENCE ANXIETY IN THEIR RELATIONSHIPS

If you have an anxiety disorder, you know it could make life much stressful than it should be. This also affects how you feel at work, while you're out with friends, and even at night. Yet anxiety can also influence the relationship by adding tension, doubt, anxiety, and the resulting mistakes and arguments.

It can be depressing to know what is worth worrying about and what is not when you see the world through an anxiety-stricken lens. This can lead you to feel confused, to shut down your claims, or to connect with your partner as passive-aggressive. Although it is not your fault, it is always helpful to remember how anxiety can affect the way you see things so that you can begin to move in a more healthy direction.

If it feels that anxiety holds you back, you might even choose to treat it for your sake. "Seeing your health care provider is one of the best things you can do when you have anxiety in your relationship," says Katie Ziskind, married and family therapist. "If you are a therapist, you'll learn positive coping skills to deal constructively with your anxiety." And this can mean a healthier relationship by avoiding some anxiety-related errors, such as:

1. Not Being Present With Your Partner (Being Absent)

One of the worst side effects of anxiety is that it is "checked out" or not fully present in your everyday life. And while this sucks itself, it can harm your relationship as well.

First of all, it can make "it hard for your partner to feel genuinely connected," says Bustle, a clinical psychologist, Dr. Paul DePompo. And so, because of these feelings of neglect, you two may have some arguments.

Nevertheless, it is an issue that can be overcome. If you are nervous, Dr.DePompo suggests you should make a conscious effort to be positive whenever you are together. You can also receive assistance from a loved one or a therapist who will show you how to cope with your fear and therefore feel more grounded.

2. Having Trust Problems

Because anxiety will make you feel like your life is being spun out of control, it is only because you won't necessarily feel safe. And this can lead to confidence problems in your relationship.

Rosalind Sedaca, a dating and relationship coach, tells Bustle: "An anxious partner can be more jealous or nervous than others to involve knowing who (their partners) are calling, texting, and

(or) meeting throughout the day." "They can telephone or email (their partner) questioning (their) behavior too often and violating (their) privacy." Although it stems from anxiety, this behavior can still affect the relationship and make your partner imagine things as follows. But this is only one more reason to seek ways of controlling anxieties and emotions so that they are not overwhelming.

Appearing as Controlling

As people who are anxious to' control' their lives frequently cope with this, "Sedacca says. And it can start leaking into your relationship, which makes you feel controlled or manipulative towards your partner. While this is not your goal, both of you can have a hard time dealing with it— especially if you have to go to treatment, learn safer ways to relieve yourself.

1. Overthinking Every Single Thing

Will you want to overthink everything? This is a massive sign of anxiety, and it can affect your trust in opening up to others— including your partner.

"The' impacts' of what you say can affect you," Dr.DePompo says. But if there is a person on the planet with whom you should be honest, it is your partner.

However, some people can get used to it with some great faith, try to stop "editing," says Dr.DePompo. It may be daunting at first, but you're certainly worth it with a supportive partner.

2. Taking Things Personal

Another side effect of anxiety is that it becomes all too easy to spring to conclusions, take the worst, and therefore take things personally.

But it's crucial not to let your partner get out of control.

74

"When[they are] distant, for example, a person with anxiety could take them personally instead of trying to have a conversation and figure out what could happen," Dr. Helen Odessky, author of Stop Anxiety From Stopping You, tells Bustle, a clinical psychologist. "Examples include stress at work, physical illness, and depression." It may be useful to train the brain, perhaps by using a therapist to first consider these external causes before jumping to conclusions and picking up fights with your partner.

3. To get "stuck" in old habits.

Relationships must be established and improved to stay healthy. Then, for someone with anxiety, this can be incredibly difficult.

"People with fear stop trying new things, taking good chances and letting go," says Dr.DePompo. "This can keep the stuff standing overnight— you need a spark to kindle a fire. If you are the type, try things irrespective of how confident they are — let it be known about the experience and shake it about the perfectionism of' the best' choices."

4. You were always Expecting Your partner To Cure Your Anxiety.

While your partner should be aware of your anxiety and be as supportive as possible, it will not help to put pressure on them to cure it.

"We want them to ease our worries or continuously comfort them, but they are not to be occupied: specifically, to take over our anxiety," said Julie Williamson, behavioral therapist, LPC, NCC, RPT, to Bustle. "This is not just not fair to your friend. It is not fair to you because your partner can not cure your fear." You can deal with yourself by taking a lot of care, making a few restful loves (like meditation or yoga), seeing a therapist, or even taking medication.

5. Replying Passive Aggressive

As anxiety may lead to feelings of irritability, you may be hitting or responding to your partner in passive-aggressive ways, says Williamson. You might also find that you can't talk to them without going downhill quickly.

6. Venting to an Unhealthy Extent

If you're not coping with your anxiety healthily, don't be surprised when you make the mistake of relieving your mate. While it's OK to let a bit of steam off and share some tense parts of your day, it can become a burden too often.

"If we feel anxious, we must be heard right away," says Bustle Melissa Kester, a marriage license and family therapist. "While we exchange a very noisy speech with all but the sink. While we are monologuing in the expectation, we'll be heard urgently. Our partner can do us." There are so many other ways to loosen that your partner's ear doesn't always have. You could go to the gym, run, call a friend, or leave everything with a therapist–everything will save your relationship.

7. Constantly Doubting the Relationship

When you continuously doubt the commitment of your partner or the safety of your partnership, it can help to step back and see if your suspicions are due to anxiety.

"People with anxiety have negative self-talk that can make them not trust that they are loved," tells

Dr.Romancé's Guide to Finding Love Today Tina B. Tessina, Ph.D., psychotherapist, and author. "This uncertainty will frustrate a partner and cause her to leave the relationship at last." To do whatever you can to reinvigorate everything is essential not only for your tranquility but also for your partner.

8. Getting Super-Angry

Like most anxious people, you can find that you are more irritable than you are. But if you're not careful, this might also snowball into anger.

"If you feel overwhelmed, trapped, and unheard of, the nervous person's reality, if you fight, can come frustration," says Kester. "When we share something important or try to stop feeling bad, our brain flips, our primitive self kicks in, we will blacks out, lose control of ourselves, and lose oral skills."

However, there are lots of healthier ways to get those thoughts out — or, first of all, to stop them. Then, therapy can be a great place to start, as can the above-described changes in lifestyle.

9. Making Big Small Problems

If you have anxiety, you may have a breakdown over small things that would not usually bother you. As Sedacca says, "Anxious partners - lead to catastrophe situations, which cause things to blow up to be more or more dangerous than what they are." This is another side effect of anxiety and can be handled through therapy. This is another side effect.

10. Avoiding conflict at all costs

One of the unproductive things in a partnership is to shut down. Yet that is what tends to happen when you battle anxiety.

"People who tend to be more nervous, tend to believe differences are evil," says Bustle's life coach, Elizabeth Su. "We often appreciate people and worry about the fact that if we disagree with our spouse, this implies that our relationship is doomed." Then, anxiety makes it difficult to see that arguments are good indeed. "What usually happens is an important conversation about something between you or both," Su says. Don't try to prevent your anxiety from engaging in productive conversations.

It would be great if you could snap your fingers and have no more anxiety, but it takes a lot of time to resolve it. But you can begin to feel better and prevent these common relationship errors by seeing a therapist, taking care of yourself, or perhaps taking medication.

CHAPTER 6
DEALING WITH RELATIONSHIP ANXIETY

As we all know, one of the most pleasurable things on the planet can be relationships, but it can as well provide a breeding ground for anxiety, feeling, and thoughts. Relationship anxiety can occur in almost any courtship stage. For many individuals, just thinking of being in a relationship will cause stress. If and when people start dating, they can have endless worries at the beginning: "Does he/she like me? "Is this going to work out? "How grave is that? "Unfortunately, in later stages of a romantic union, these concerns are not eased. Yes, anxiety can get even more serious as things get closer between a couple. Thoughts flow like this: "Can this be the last? "Do I like him/her?" Ought we to slow down? "Am I ready for such an engagement?" Does he/she lose interest?"

We can feel pretty lonely with all this thinking about our relationships, and it can bring about a distance between you and your partner. At its worst, our anxiety can even lead us to give up entirely on love. Understanding and knowing more about the causes and effects of sex anxiety can help us identify the negatives that can undermine our lives of passion. How can we control our anxiety and be vulnerable to someone we love?

What Causes Anxiety in Relationships?

Simply put, falling in love challenges us in many ways that we don't expect. The more we love another, the more we lose. We are afraid of being hurt in many ways, both conscious and unconscious. To some extent, we all have a fear of intimacy. Interestingly, this anxiety always comes when we get exactly what we want, and when we experience love as never before or when we are handled unfamiliarly.

When we get into a relationship, we are not just nervous about the things happening between ourselves and our partner; they are the things we tell ourselves about what is happening. The "sensitive internal voice" is a term used to describe our mean coach who criticizes us, gives us bad advice, and fuels our fear of intimacy. It says to us:

- "You are too ugly/fat/boring to hold an interest."

- \"You're never going to meet anyone, so why even try?

- "You can't believe him. He is looking for someone way better."

- "She doesn't love you. He's looking for someone better." Get out before you get hurt.

We turn against ourselves and the people near us through that critical inner voice. It can foster aggressive, negative, and suspicious thinking, thereby decreasing self-esteem, and increasing unhealthy levels of suspicion, denial, envy, and fear. In essence, it feeds us on a constant stream of thoughts, which undermines our happiness, and we ended up with worries about our relationship instead of just enjoying it.

If we dwell on those concerned feelings, we are utterly diverted from real relationships with our partner. We can start to act in destructive ways, comment badly, or become childish or parental towards others. Think of your partner staying late at work one night, for instance. Sitting alone at home, the inner critic begins to say, "Where is she? Would you truly trust her? Perhaps she wants to be away from you; she tries to avoid you, and she does not love you anymore. "Such feelings will snowball in your mind until you feel insecure, frustrated, or suspicious when your partner comes home. You can be angry or cold, which then frustrates and protects your friend. You changed the dynamic between you too early. Instead of spending time together, you may waste a whole night feeling withdrawn and upset. You forced the gap you were initially afraid of. The fault behind this theory is not the situation itself; this vital inner voice influenced your thought, skewed your beliefs, and guided you along a destructive path.

When all the issues that we worry about in relationships are involved, we are more resilient than we think. In truth, we can deal with the hurts and refusals that we fear so much. We can feel pain and gradually recover. The vital inner voice, however, tends to terrorize and disaster the truth. It can cause severe anxiety about non-existent dynamics and threats that aren't even tangible. Even when things happen, someone breaks with us or has an interest in someone else; our vital inner voice will tear us apart in ways that we do not deserve. This utterly distorts reality and destroys our power and determination. This pessimistic roommate also offers terrible advice. "You cannot live. You cannot survive this". Always put your guard up and never be vulnerable to anybody else. We have our own unique experience and adaptations in the protections we create and the critical voices we hear. If we are nervous or insecure, some of us tend to cling to our actions and be desperate. We may feel possessed or controlled in response to our partner. On the other side, some of us will quickly feel intruded in our ties. We will withdraw from our friends and separate ourselves from our feelings of desire. We can act aloof, remote, or guarded. These relationship patterns can come from our styles of early attachment. This design of attachment is formed in childhood attachments. It remains a working model for adult relationships, which eventually affects how every one of us responds to our needs and how we fulfill them. Various attachment types can contribute to multiple levels of anxiety about relationships.

What Thoughts Perpetuate Anxiety In Relationships?

The specific critical inner-voices we have about ourselves, our partners, and our relationships are made up of our early attitudes in our family and society as a whole. Sexual assumptions and attitudes towards oneself and others that our influential caretakers had will invade our current perceptions. While the inner criticism of all is different, some of the common critical inner voices are:

Critical inner voices about relationship

- Relationships never work out

- People end up getting hurt

Voice about your partner

- Men are so unreliable, selfish and insensitive

- Women are so vulnerable, needy and indirect

- He doesn't care about you; he only cares about his friends

- You can't trust her

- What is so great about her, anyway? Why so

excited

- He cannot get anything right in his life

- He's probably cheating on you

Voices about yourself:

- It is not your fault if he gets upset

- You will never find someone who understands you.

- Don't get too stuck on it. Don't get too hooked on her

- He doesn't care about you

- She is too perfect for you

- You can only get him interested

- You are better off without her

- She will reject you as soon as she gets to know you.

- You must be in control.

- Don't be too weak or just get hurt.

How Does Anxiety in Relationship Affect Us?

When we shine a light on our history, we quickly realize that our attachment pattern, psychological defenses, and vital inner voices have had many early influences. All these factors contribute to our distress and can, in many ways, ruin our lives of happiness. Hearing our inner criticism and contributing to this discomfort will lead to the following measures:

- *Cling:* If we are concerned, our inclination may be to behave towards our partner aggressively. We may cease to feel like the independent, strong people we were when we became involved. As a result, we can easily break apart, act jealously or unsafe, or no longer participate in independent activities.

- *Control:* We can try to control our partner when we feel threatened. We can and cannot make rules just to ease our feelings of insecurity or anxiety. This can alienate our partner and create anger.

- *Reject:* if we are worried about our relationship, we might turn to aloofness for one's defense. We may get cold or refuse to protect ourselves or attack our partner. Subtle or transparent, these acts are almost always a sure way of forcing distance or generating uncertainty in our partner.

- **_Withhold:_** We often prefer to withhold from our partner, unlike overt denial, when we are nervous or afraid. Perhaps things got close, and we feel stirred up, so we're going to escape. We have little love or completely give up on some part of our relationship. Withholding may look like a passive act, yet in a relationship, it is one of the quietest killers of passion and attraction.

- **_Threaten:_** Our reaction to our distress is sometimes more violent, and we punish our partner. We can either shout or give the cold shoulder to our partner. It is essential to be careful of how our actions respond to our partner and how they respond to our critical inner voice.

- **_Retreat:_** When we are scared in a relationship, we can give up genuine intimacy and retreat into a "fantasy relationship." In this fantasy state, we concentrate on shape over substance. We stay in connection to feel safe, but we give up the essential parts of the relationship. Often in a fantasy bond, we engage in many of the above destructive behaviors as a means of distancing ourselves and defending ourselves from the anxiety that is, of course, free and loving.

How Can I Overcome Anxiety in Relationships?

To conquer the anxiety of relationships, we need to shift our focus inward. We have to see what's happening within us, independent of our partner or the relationship. What critical internal voices intensify our fears? What defenses do we have that can create distance? This self-discovery process can be a vital step in understanding the feelings which drive our actions and finally form our relationship. Through looking at our history, we will gain a better understanding of the origins of these emotions. What made us feel confused or turned on about love? You can start the journey for yourself by learning more about the fear of intimacy and how your vital inner voice can be recognized and addressed.

CHAPTER 7
OVERCOMING JEALOUSY IN A RELATIONSHIP

Ending jealousy is like altering every mental or behavioral response. It begins with consciousness. Awareness lets you see that the predicted stories are not real in your head. If you are so straightforward, you no longer respond to the possibilities your imagination might imagine. Jealousy and anger are emotional reactions that are not true in believing situations in your head. You should change what you think affects what your imagination projects and remove these harmful emotional reactions. Even if the reaction is warranted, envy and rage are not good ways to cope with the situation and to get what we want—trying to change anxiety or resentment when you feel like controlling a car skidding on ice. Your ability to deal with the situation will greatly improve if you can clear the risk before we get there. This means addressing the beliefs that cause jealousy rather than trying to control your emotions.

Dissolving relationships permanently means changing the underlying beliefs of fear and unconscious expectations of what the partner is doing.

The steps to end jealous reactions permanently are:

1. Recover personal power so that you can control your emotions and stop reactive behavior.

2. Change your point of view so you can step back from your plot; this gives you a gap of time to avoid a jealous or angry reaction and to do something else.

3. Identify the core convictions that trigger the emotional response.

4. Be mindful that your convictions are not valid; this is distinct from scientifically "knowing" that the claims are not real.

5. Gain power over your focus so that you can actively select your mind's story and emotions.

Several factors establish the envy dynamic. As such, practical solutions will tackle multiple elements of values, experiences, feelings, and strength of personal will. You will leave the doors open to those negative emotions and behaviors if you lack one or more of these components.

You can step back from the story by practicing some simple exercises and refrain from the emotional reaction. If you want to change your feelings and actions, you can do it. It only takes the readiness to acquire sufficient skills.

Principle triggers of jealousy are convictions that create insecurity feelings.

Low self-esteem based on convictions of who we are. To eradicate fear and low self-esteem, we do not have to change our confidence in the false self-image. While some people believe this may be difficult, it's only tricky because most people haven't learned the skills needed to change their faith. When you practice your skills, it takes minimal effort to change a belief. You just stop thinking about the story. It takes more energy than it does to believe something.

Self-Judgment May Intensify the Feeling Of Insecurity

It is not enough to "learn" the emotion intellectually. Only in this way will the Inner Judge abuse us with criticism of what we do. The Interior Judge could use this knowledge to push us into more vulnerability by an emotional downward spiral. Then, you have to develop skills to dissolve beliefs and falsified self-images and to control your mind projects. The practices and skills of the audio sessions are available. The first and second sessions are free and should give us an idea of how the mind works to create emotions. Sessions 1 and 2 also give you great exercises to regain some personal power and adjust your feelings.

One of the steps to changing behavior is to see how we create the emotion of wrath or jealousy from our minds. This very step will not only allows us to take responsibility but also puts us in a position to change our emotions.

We don't take responsibility if we're in a relationship with a jealous partner and might want to change your behavior to avoid envy. Saying things like, "When you wouldn't, then I wouldn't react like this." This kind of language flags a powerless attitude and attempts to control your behavior by dealing with it.

How The Mind Produces The Emotions Of Anger And Jealousy

I described in the description below the mechanism of jealousy and anger. When you try to overcome envy, you probably already know the complexities I explain. This explanation can help to fill the holes in how the mind turns knowledge into self-judgment and increases low self-esteem and insecurity. This theoretical understanding will contribute to the development of consciousness to see these complexities when you do so. But you need a different set of skills to make effective changes. You don't have enough details about how you build your emotional reactions. Just like realizing you have a flat tire, you didn't know how to patch the tire because you stumbled over the screw.

I will use a guy as a jealous companion for the example. I am talking about different pictures in mind, and you can refer to the chart below or see the Relationship Matrix for a more detailed description of these images.

It starts with a man who feels nervous. Insecurity stems from his "not perfect" False Hidden Image. The man creates self-rejection in his mind because he believes that this false image is who he is rather than a picture in his mind. The mental consequence of self-rejection is a feeling of indignity, vulnerability, apprehension, and unhappiness.

Compensating for Fear

To overcome the emotion created as a result of the hidden false image, he concentrates on his perceived positive qualities to counteract the feeling created by his secret model. From these attributes, the man will create a false image of himself. I call this the Projected Picture because he needs to be seen like this. The mental consequence of a positive self-image is not self-rejection or indignity. There is greater acceptance, and he generates more love and happiness. Notice that he has not changed; depending on the moment, he only has a different image in his mind.

The hidden image belief causes unhappiness, while the projected image causes more pleasant emotions. It must be remembered that both pictures are fake. Both images are in the mind of the man, and nobody is him. He is the one who creates and reacts in his imagination to the images. In his vision, he's not an image.

The mind of the man blends the projected image with the qualities attracted by women. The characteristics are often considered positive because women are attracted to them. When a man receives attention from a woman, he links himself to the projected image instead of the image "Not Good Enough." The increased trust in the projected image leads to more social acceptance, love, and happiness.

It is the recognition and loving behavior of a man that changes his emotional state. The image or the attention of the woman does not change his emotion. These are only triggers that activate the mind of the man towards specific values, acceptance of himself, and love.

The mind of the man also makes the idea "she makes him happy" or "needs" it to be glad. It only appears this way because he notices the relationship between the woman and her emotional state. The man often does not know that his mind is only an emotional tool to express love. He may not have developed other opportunities to communicate his acceptance and love, so he relies on a woman for a catalyst. If the man realized that she is only a trigger and that his role in expressing acceptance and love changed his emotional state, the man did not "need" his partner to be happy.

The contradictory False Images of the man may look in his mind like this.

Control Behavior

The man operates by the misconception that he is happier because of the attention and love of a woman. If he thinks that her attention is focused on someone or something else, he responds with terror. The main fear is not to lose the woman as he may believe falsely. The main concern is to stop the emotional pain that the secret picture produces in his head.

His Hidden Image convictions become true without his knowledge. His perception of himself also contributes to an understanding of this "not good enough" situation. His feeling of indignity and unhappiness reflects his convictions and perspective.

The man tries to get and monitor the attention of the woman so that the trust in the projected image is active. He works to "activate" his "trigger" to support his belief in the projected image. It's the way that he uses to escape his Hidden Image beliefs. He does not know that love and acceptance are the keys to change his emotional state.

Punishment and Anger to Control Behavior

One of the mechanisms which we learn early in life is the regulation of the attention and actions of others through anger. When we were disciplined as infants, this punishment was often followed by rage. Often harsh words were enough to make us change our behavior. This got our attention, at least when someone was upset with us. So we learned early in life to use wrath to control the recognition of others and to punish the behavior of other people. We didn't necessarily unlearn this trend when we grew older.

The jealous man uses his partner's rage to get his attention and to control it. Anger sometimes serves as a justification for the woman's emotional pain. The woman can change her behavior by punishing the woman with anger to avoid emotional punishment in the future.

The wrath of the man may not be his favorite choice. Yet his rage behavior is the product of a false paradigm of belief. The man can "think" differently in his mind, but his conduct rests upon false convictions and a distorted picture that drives his emotions.

The Actual Outcome Of Controlling Anger

The man gets the opposite results of his anger as a child. An adult has more power to resist the punishment of rage than a child. The woman will withdraw due to her tendency to avoid emotional disagreement. Her retirement will then trigger her confidence in the distorted picture he tried to prevent. The creed-emotion process of the man comes back to the beginning. This is painful emotionally.

Analysis After the Incident

The study after the incident, there is an opportunity to look at and evaluate events after a jealousy and rage incident. This period can be emotionally more difficult for the jealous man. His self-assurance can be the worst of all.

The man plays the action of rage and power in his mind. However, it is now examined by the Inner Judge. The Interior Judge analyzes the matter and condemns him. The inner judge holds the projected image explicitly and then points out that he has failed to fulfill this standard. He can only assume that he's a loser and not good enough based on the predicted picture level.

The rage case, seen by the Inner Judge, is "proof" that he is the person, in the fact that fits the description of the Hidden Picture. Accepting this judgment and believing it, the man feels unworthy, guilty, and disgraceful. The Inner Judge enhances the belief, feeling, and perception of the character of the secret image. It's a suspended lawyer. The judge does not evaluate the role of the belief system, false images, or the viewpoint. The man is at the hands of powers, which he was not educated to see and deal with. He can begin to control his emotional state with an awareness of these forces and certain specific practices.

Attempts to change behavior do not seem to work.

The main problem in the study is that man approaches the events from a judgmental point of view. Judgment leads to denial. It also serves to improve confidence in the standard of perfection. This view strengthens the Hidden Image and the belief that the projected image is a core cause. The very thing in our mind that the research is doing is merely enhancing the core causes.

A man looks for a solution, and the solution seems to become the' Projected Image' in this paradigm of indignity. But then, if he can become the confident, strong, kind, and loving person he knows he is, he will love himself, the woman will love him, and everything will be fine. He doesn't see that his imagination forms the projected image.

This strategy has other issues.

1. The man's conviction that he is the Projected Image is being undermined by his conviction that he is not "strong enough." Being perfect may sometimes compensate, but the sense of unworthiness passes until the hidden image is addressed.

2. Even if the man turns out to be the perfect projected image, the hidden faith in the image will feel like a fraud. He's not really "good," and he's not "worthy," according to Hidden picture beliefs. He'll be unauthentic because of these conflicting beliefs. The sensation of being a cheat also arises when others applaud his achievements. The more

successful and recognizable he is, the more prominent is the hidden image in his mind. It can't be emotionally integrated as long as he combines his identity with one or more conflicting images in his mind.

3. The efforts of the man to control his emotion will protect him from the eruption of jealousy and anger. This "on watch" feeling emerges out of the fear that emotion will consume his attention at any time. Not only does that feeling of fear affect a person, but it also represses emotions and does not allow true love and joy to be felt.

4. Strong positive values and a positive self-image can, but to a certain degree, help to reduce the reaction side. It is a patch that can support but still find identity in a false picture, not in honesty and dignity. He does nothing to resolve the feelings that are at the center of the actions from the distorted thoughts or the convictions of unworthiness. These are often hidden in the subconscious and then come back during times of stress when they are most harmful.

False Beliefs and Emotion Drive the Behavior

When one looks at the conduct of jealousy and anger as a means of controlling and holding others, the action makes no sense. Wrath and envy won't make anyone closer to us. The man can often look at his behavior in the situation and see that it makes no sense. As a result of his actions, he can see the woman leaving him. Seeing the outcome and knowing it intellectually, however, does not change its behavioral dynamic. Why? Why?

His conduct is not motivated by thought, reasoning, or analytical understanding. Therefore, It can not be modified by these modalities. It is guided by beliefs, false images, opinions, and emotions. If we are to change our behavior, these basic elements must be discussed in a way other than pure intelligence and logic. Why do you use a different approach to intellect and logic? Intellect and reasoning will be used by the Interior Judge to make decisions and improve the current false beliefs.

Going By the Results

Changing attitudes, emotional reactions, and destructive behavior are by overcoming the false beliefs of your mind, your focus, and your point of view. When you learn to change your perspective, you can move away from confidence and emotion. From a new perspective, you are aware of the wrong logic of the beliefs behind your behavior. You will be in a position to refrain from destructive behavior, recognizing the false beliefs behind your actions. Eliminating misconceptions eliminates emotional triggers. It is the elimination of false convictions that will remove fear.

If you want to change a jealous and angry behavior, you will have to do more than study the issue. You're going to have to move. I propose to continue with the free audio sessions. Practice the exercises for a couple of days and hear what you know. You will register free of charge. No credit card details are needed.

HOW TO OVERCOME JEALOUSY IN A RELATIONSHIP

Jealousy is not totally a bad thing; it's human nature. From time to time, it is natural to feel jealous.

Envy is troublesome "when we behave or wallow out in envy," says Christina Hibbert, PsyD, Flagstaff, clinical psychologist, Ariz.

It becomes complicated when he starts to overwhelm you and "creates into every part of your life," said Kathy Morelli, LPC, a psychotherapist with a specialty of marriage and family therapy in Wayne, N.J.

Romantic jealousy is one of the most common forms of jealousy, she said. They are also jealous of the successes, talents, lifestyles, and relationships of others, Hibbert said.

For example, we may think that the life of someone is much easier or more comfortable than ours. "We only see good and only evil in our life." Or maybe we assume that our best friend has a better relationship with another friend.

Social networking sites like Facebook can also cause envy. Today, our online and offline worlds overlap, and relationships and similarities are much more complicated and nuanced, "said Morelli.

Insecurity is often the basis of jealousy. "We're feeling threatened, or less or insufficiently healthy," said Hibbert. We fear that the abilities of somebody else mean something bad about us." (Also, jealously maybe a product of your previous experiences, but more later). Below, there will be general tips for coping with envy, together with concrete jealousy suggestions in romantic relations.

Romantic Relationship Tips

\-   **Evaluate your relationship**

"Great way to overcome insecurity is to look at your romantic relationship first," said Morelli. Consider, for example, if your relationship is based on honesty, respect, and love, and if the actions of your partner represent their expressions.

Were they honest with you, were they honest? If you are not, this can cause or sustain your insecurities, said

Morelli, who also writes the books BirthTouch ® for pregnant and postpartum couples, Perinatal Childbirth Professional Mental Illness and Healing for NICU Parents.

"When you are in an unstable relationship, expect your jealousy buttons to be pressed. But no one can say what to do to you. Sometimes, you may feel bad and jealous if you stay. "Assess yourself.

- **Evaluate Yourself**

If you have a safe and strong relationship, and still feel jealous, look at yourself and explore your own experiences.

"Research in a romantic relationship on the topic of envy indicates that a person's fundamental style of attachment underlies their susceptibility to jealous reactions," Morelli said.

Individuals who in their early years have developed stable relationships between themselves and their careers, appear to be less protective and dependent thereby have greater autonomy, and have fewer feelings of insufficiency than children in unstable attachment styles.

Morelli asked himself the following questions:

- Do you have an intense sense of emptiness or lack of self-esteem?

- Were your early caregivers not reliable?

- Were you raised in a repressive environment?

- What's your relationship with your early caregivers?

- Do you feel a lack of self-worth or pervasive feeling?

- Was the environment you were raised warm and loving and also critical?

The type of attachment is malleable, she said. Subsequent interactions and conditions will affect your style. For example, a professional therapist can help you develop self-esteem and deal with your issues.

Seek other support

Morelli said, have interests beyond your partnership. Discuss with a friend about your jealous sensations, "but don't do this to the exclusion of talking with your partner."

General Tips

-       Always recognize your jealousy

"It loses its control when we call envy because we're no longer letting it intimidate us," said Hibbert. Recognizing you're jealous, she said, opens the door to understanding.

-   Learn from your jealousy

Hibbert, the author of the book "This Is How We Grow," said we could use feelings of envy as a motivation to grow. You know, for example, that every time your friend plays his guitar, you get jealous because you want to do it too. Instead of wallowing in that envy, you sign up for guitar lessons, she said.

-   Let it go

Tell yourself that in your life, you don't need that feeling, so you give it up, said Hibbert. Then "respire deeply and imagine it flowing like the wind through you. Repeat as often as you need to quit it. "Healthily control your feelings.

- **Manage your emotions**

"Practice consciousness to soothe the weakening feelings," said Morelli. For starters, she recommended that readers tap into your body to see how you feel, take some deep breaths, and try to separate yourself from the strength of these emotions.

She said, if your envy concerns your romantic relationship, once you calm down, share your feelings with your partner.

She also suggested journaling, dancing, and listening to your favorite music to channel your feelings.

- **Remind yourself of your positive features**

"She's very good at playing with her kids, and I'm not so sweet. Hibbert gave this example. But I'm great at reading to them, and they love me. "She said that she teaches everyone that everybody has strengths and weaknesses.

Jealousy is, once again, a normal reaction. When it becomes chronic, it becomes troublesome. Recognize what happens when you feel jealous and deepen your relationships and yourself.

CHAPTER 8
RESOLVING CONFLICTS IN YOUR RELATIONSHIP

You are sitting in a cafeteria. Two couples sit near you in the store. The couple on the left argue if they want to go with friends for dinner. She says, "The last time you said so to me, it's never fun," She answers: "Of course you'd like to say that because they're my friends, and you've never offered another friend a chance." War and peace, our personal edition, whatever number. "They turn away and sit in silence.

The couple on the right often explore whether they want to go with friends to have dinner. He says, "I think I'm a bit worried it'll go on for hours and it couldn't be that interesting. What do you think? What do you think?" She replies," Hey, even I know that happens. You know Jim; the only person who likes to talk more than he is... oh, wait! That's me! That's me!" He smiles and says,' Yeah, but I like listening to you speak. Tom, not so much.

To him, I get a bit bored–not you. She says, "I get that, I want to go, but perhaps we can arrange a time when we must leave as a compromise?" Apart from that, it will be good to get home early enough to have a great time to enjoy the rest of our night together." He smiles and nods, and they keep on reading and enjoying their coffee.

Both couples had a conflict–in fact, the same one. One responded by using bad habits and used the struggle to widen a distance between them. The other used conflict as an incentive for their relationship to expand and develop. Does that couple think you have the best and most successful relationship? What partnership will last longer, do you think? You should look at how you and your partner handle conflicts if you are looking to understand how to save your relationship from breaking up.

Conflict Can Be Destructive

Conflict with your spouse can make you feel attacked or threatened, vulnerable and weak, and so draw you back and back. When you believe that your partner is upset, you are less likely to react constructively and more likely to turn to old staff like "silent therapy," which is harmful than healthy. This will eventually break down the friendship.

If someone asked you if you understood how to resolve the conflict, you would probably say yes. If they asked you when quiet treatment was an appropriate way to deal with the conflict, you would nearly say no. Then, you know better than to resort to these dumb tactics, but you do so anyway if you are wounded enough. Why? Why? Why reject negative patterns instead of working to fix the communication problems?

How Conflict Can Emerge

Break the pattern of aggression and give positive energy to conflict. Don't get defensive, don't hammer the case, and don't try winning. Why would you like to lose your friend, the one you love?

Conflicts provide you and your partners with opportunities to align values and results. We are chances of knowing, appreciating, and embracing disparities. Place yourself in the role of your partner and try to understand his perspective. Such interactions and feelings may be painful, but we can never develop if we always choose comfort.

A great tactic is to use humor to break the pattern if you find yourself in a retaliatory spiral. Attempt to compete with Christopher Walken or William Shatner. Make the conflict funny.

Let's go back to the coffee shop to illustrate this point. You see an elderly couple. The man spills his tea across the table by mistake and then splashes and drips onto his wife's favorite outfit. He's got some napkins out, and she's laughing and joking aloud to other customers, "He's doing this to me for 20 years— never finished a cup before!" He returns, dabs her tea and jokes back to the other bosses," she asked! "She asked for it!" They both laugh, you and everybody else in the shop do too. Many people would have converted the situation into fights, but with laughter, this husband and wife took a moment to nip the retaliatory spiral in his bud and turned it into an opportunity for them to laugh, enjoy and escape the argument.

Humor is a solution to solving problems in relationships. It can relieve stress and allow you and your partner to concentrate instead of what you both want.

What do you want? What are you supposed to focus on? Remember to add, not to subtract. Every one of our partners does stuff or has habits, which bothers us. Alternatively, concentrate on what you bring to the table, how you feel, and what you enjoy. You'll find that even those things that drive you crazy are soon going to miss because they're part of the whole person, your partner, whom you love.

Use conflict as a means of aligning your values and objectives, and of injecting passion and energy into your relationship. Remember the two coffee couples? The productive couple who put their energies in knowing the needs of each other reaffirmed their love for each other—supported the need to leave at a certain time and supported their need to socialize with friends. They also played it as a compromise and promised to go home early enough to spend time together in quality.

Listen to your partner, understand what they say and why they feel like doing. Be truthful with your own emotions and feelings. Be your true self, as the conflict is a real opportunity to connect with your partner.

Conflict is also an opportunity to find out more and

love your partner even deeper. This is a chance to add spark and take your relationship to the next level. Prepare to see disagreements as changes to something better rather than as excuses to withdraw. Next time you disagree with your partner and discuss how to save your relationship, choose to see the world favorably in the case instead of the negative and take an active decision to work together toward a more stable future.

How to Create New Habits

You must be constructive to make it happen, particularly if you have to overcome your hurt feelings to figure out how to correct your relationship. You may have an exceptional store of information, skills, and resources, but the point is moot if you do not have the desire to use them.

We appear to retaliate and to react with more hate to aggression, which produces a vicious cycle that amplifies and increases a conflict's negativity. This is called the cycle of revenge and can lead to a friendship and, ultimately, an end. You have negative self-sabotage patterns.

What causes this? When you focus on protecting yourself from attack rather than solving the problem that would help solve the relationship challenges, a dispute becomes negative. By focusing on your suffering and pain, you are making sure that you experience more of the same, as you do not put your energy into one that avoids suffering and pain: looking for solutions to help you learn how to save your relationship.

Years ago, Tony Robbins took an isolated two-lane highway lined only at intervals of 10 to 20 yards with power lines. One seemed perpetually decorated in a particular snake-like area of the road with flowers, candles, and photographs memorializing and honoring the life of the victims of the road that struck the post. Then, with so much space on either side of the post, how many people were killed or wounded hit, it was incredible. Why was it not evaded by the victim? Why have they not swerved to either side?

It's because people's attention would be on not touching the stick. However, our focus is on our direction. In case we don't want to hit the pole, we must concentrate on what we want: steer the car to each side of the pole.

118

We can change the result by shifting our emphasis. Your relationship is the lesson. You will find your relationship where you don't want it to end, to struggle or get upset. Either in a miserable, unfulfilling relationship or split from your partner, you will find yourself where you don't want to be. When you concentrate on conflict resolution and evolving together, you will focus on the goals you want and achieve them. Intend to connect well with your friend. If both of you are satisfied and happy, then you have the tools to build a beautiful, passionate, and lasting relationship. Where emphasis flows, flows of energy.

You can turn a disagreement from something wrong into an opportunity to take your relationship to the next level by shifting your viewpoints and emphasis. It includes focus, which you are now advancing and practicing. You learn not to respond with aggression, but with positive measures to improve the relationship.

Turning Conflict into Something Positive

Break the pattern and give positive energy to conflict. Don't get defensive, pound the case; don't try to win. Why would you like to lose your friend, the one you love? If you accept that there are no losers in love and you want to win together, you can focus on letting go of small arguments and be on good communication.

Conflicts offer you and your partners the opportunity to align values and results. We are chanced of knowing, appreciating, and embracing disparities. Sit in and try to understand your partner's experience; this is how you learn to maintain a relationship. Such interactions and feelings can be painful, but we can never develop if we always opt for comfort.

Use Your Humor to Diffuse The Situation

When you find yourself in a retaliatory loop, a good tactic is to use humor to break the pattern. Take a moment to pause if you sense an argument escalating. Try to argue like Christopher Walken or Shatner. Sing a song that causes your partner to laugh. Render the dispute amusing.

So, let us now go back to the case of the cafeteria to explain this. You see an elderly couple. Accidentally, the man throws his tea around the table and splashes on the favorite dress of his friend. He's gotten ready for some treats and laughs and jokes aloud to other customers, "I've been doing it for twenty years–he's never done a cup yet!" He comes back, takes her tea off, and laughs to the other managers," she asked for it!" We both chuckle, and together with everybody else in the shop, you do too. Many people would have turned the situation into an argument, but with humor, this husband and wife took a moment to nip the retaliatory spiral in the bud and convert it into an opportunity to joke and to enjoy.

Humor is a Steppingstone to Solving Relationship Issues

It can alleviate stress and allow you and your partner to concentrate on what you and your partner both want, such as a caring and happy relationship–rather than what you want, a needless dispute.

Once you know how to repair your relationship, you need to ask yourself some questions: What do you want? What are you supposed to focus on? Try to admire, not to weaken. Even our friends do stuff or have habits that bother us because there is no perfect human being. Instead of focusing on your bad habits or negative behaviors, concentrate on what they have to offer, how they make you feel, and what you enjoy. You will realize that you're soon going to miss even the things that made you nuts because they belong to the whole person you love, your friend.

Be the Best You Can be For Your Partner

Are you the best for your partner? Are you wondering, "How can I save my relationship?" Use conflict as an opportunity to align your beliefs and priorities, and to instill in your relationship passion and energy. Remember the two coffee couples? The positive couple, who put energy into recognizing the need of each other, expressed their support–supported their need to leave within an hour and supported their need to speak to friends. They communicated with each other; they evaluated each other's needs and made it fun to resolve rather than allow anything small to become a major argument. They even approached it as a compromise and promised to return home early enough to have a good time together.

Listen, understand what your partner is saying, and why they feel the way they do. Be honest with your own emotions and feelings. Be your authentic self, as conflict should not be seen as the end of a relationship; otherwise great; see conflict as a way to connect with your partner.

Instead of seeing conflict as a challenge to your

partner's relationship, see it as a positive tool. Conflict is also an avenue to learn more and appreciate your partner evermore. It's a chance to add passion and bring your relationship to the next level. Learn to consider conflicts as transitions to something better rather than as reasons for retreating. When you next disagree and ask how to save your relationship, choose to see the positive rather than the negative and consciously decide to work together for a more stable future.

GREAT TIPS IN SOLVING RELATIONSHIP CONFLICTS

As everyone who has been in a romantic relationship knows, disagreements and struggles are inevitable. If two people spend a lot of time together, entangled with their lives, they are expected to disagree sometimes. Such differences can be large or small, from what to eat for dinner to whether the pair should move to a job or focus on childhood religious upbringing.

The mere fact that you clash with your partner is not an indication that your relationship is troubled. In reality, fighting will strengthen your relationship when handled properly. You'll never fix them if you never fight and never think about your problems. You can better understand your partner and arrive at a solution that works for both of you by dealing with conflicts constructively. On the other hand, disputes can also intensify and generate ill will without anything being resolved. How can you improve the chances of effective conflict resolution in your relationship? Here are ten tips supported by research:

1. Be direct

Often, people don't just go out and clearly tell what disturbs them but instead choose more subtle ways to express disgust. One person may talk to the other in a way that's condescending and suggests underlying animosity. Sometimes, partners will mope and pout without really solving a problem. Partners can also avoid solving a question by moving subjects quickly when this issue arises or by ignoring it. These indirect ways of communicating wrath are not helpful, as they do not give a clear indication of how to respond to the person who is the object of behavior. They know that their partner is upset, but they do not have any instructions on what they can do to resolve the problem.

2. Talk about how you feel without your partner being blamed.

Statements that directly attack the character of your partner can harm the relationship, most especially if a man is upset with the envy of his partner, saying, "You're irrational." A more proactive approach is to use a declaration and pair it with compliance descriptions.' The statements concentrate on how you feel without criticizing your partner, and comportment descriptions focus on a particular behavior that your partner does not have a character defect. For instance, this man might say,' I'm irritated when you say that during an innocent conversation, I flirt with someone.' These are direct tactics, but they do not challenge the character of your partner.

It should be noted that in some situations, these direct negative tactics can be constructive. Research showed that blaming and denying a partner during a conflict discussion was associated with less satisfaction in a relationship over time and tended to make problems worse for couples with relatively minor problems. A different picture emerged for couples with major problems: blame and rejection attitudes directly after the dispute resolution contributed to less satisfaction, but the problems changed over the long term, and this resulted in an increase in relationship satisfaction.

3. Never say never

You should avoid generalizing your partner when dealing with a problem. Statements such as "you never help yourself" or "you always look at your mobile phone" will probably make you defensive. Instead of encouraging a dialogue on how your partner can be more helpful or more cautious, this approach would probably lead your partner to produce counter-examples of all occasions when they were helpful or careful. Also, you don't want your defensive partner.

4. Choose your fights

You have to stick to one issue at a time if you want a constructive debate. Unhappy pairs can pull several subjects into one discussion, a well-known conflict researcher, John Gottman, calls it "kitchen sinking." It refers to the old term "all but the sink," which means that everything was integrated. If you want to solve your problems, this is probably not your strategy. Imagine thinking about incorporating more physical exercise into your daily routine. You certainly wouldn't decide this would be a perfect time to think about saving more money for retirement, organizing your wardrobe, and figuring out how to manage an uncomfortable situation at work. You'd try to solve these problems one by one. This seems to be simple, but the battle over one theme can turn into a yelling session in the heat of an argument when both partners exchange gripes. However, the more complaints you raise, the less likely it is that anyone will be discussed and resolved in full.

5. Listen to your partner.

It can be somewhat frustrating to feel that you don't pay attention to your partner. When you interrupt your friend or presume you know what they think, you don't allow them to express themselves. You can still feel like you are not listening, even if you are sure where your partner is from, or know what he'll say. You can prove that you're paying attention through active listening techniques. As your partner talks, paraphrase what he's saying–that's your own words. This can prevent misconceptions before they begin. You can also test your interpretation by ensuring that you correctly interpret the reactions of your partner. For example, "You seem annoyed by that — am I correct?" Such techniques avoid confusion and show your partner that you pay attention and care about what they say.

6. Don't automatically object to complaints from your partner.

It's tough not to get angry if you're attacked. But it doesn't solve problems with defensiveness. Imagine a couple arguing because their wife wants her husband to do more housework. If she suggests that he does a quick cleaning when he gets ready to leave in the morning, he says, "Yeah, that's going to be helpful, but I don't have time in the morning." When she says that he's going to reserve for a while at the weekend, he says, "Sure, that could be a way to arrange it, but normally, we have weekends, and I'm working so it won't work." Another negative and protective behavior, when you respond to one of your partners' grievances, is "cross-complaining." In answer to"you're not cleaning up enough around the house," for example, with "You're a sweet freak."

However, you must listen to your partner and respect what they mean.

7. Take a different view

While listening to your friend, you have to consider their point of view and try to understand where they come from. Those who can take their partner's viewpoint are less likely to become frustrated in a conflict discussion.

Other research has shown that it can be helpful to take a more objective approach. The researchers conducted a simple marital quality intervention in one study, which asked participants to write about a certain disagreement they had with their partners from a neutral- third party who wanted the best for the two partners. Couples who went on this 20-minute writing, three times a year, kept the marital satisfaction steady during the year, while couples who did not show decreases in satisfaction.

8. Don't disdain your partner

Of all the negative things that you can do in a fight, the worst could be disdain. Gottman considered it to be the indicator number one of divorce. Disdainful comments are the ones that are insulting your spouse. Sarcasm and name-calling may be involved. It can also include non-verbal conduct, such as rolling or smirking of your eyes. This action is highly disrespectful, and it means the partner is disgusting.

Suppose one partner says, "I wish you took me out more," and the other partner replies, "Oh yeah, the most important thing to be seen and treated is to pay too heavy a price for small parts of food in a rip-off restaurant. Could you be more superficial?

9. Don't become distracted by negativity

It may be difficult not to answer the bad behavior of a partner with even worse behavior. Nonetheless, encouraging this desire will only intensify the conflict. In case you and your partner poor reciprocity consequences, i.e., they are constantly exchanging angry insults and contemptuous remarks. So how much is pessimistic too much? Gottman found in his study that the magic number is a relation from five to one: people with five positive behaviors (for example, attempts at a good mood, warmth, and cooperation) were significantly less likely to have split or separated from each negative behavior four years later.

10. Know what time for a time-out is right

When you find that you or your partner do not meet the above instructions, consider taking some time off from your claims. A short time out to take a breath is somewhat adequate to relax hot temperament. Conflict research shows that taking into account and managing your frustration is the secret to adequately coping with disputes. It can be constructive in your relationship to resolve your problems, but disputes must be properly managed, or you risk exacerbating them.

CHAPTER 9

HOW TO OVERCOME OVERTHINKING IN A RELATIONSHIP/MARRIAGE

I believe that we are all over-thinkers, regardless of whether or not we are conscious, and that is another problem. I used to overthink everything; it was like a good feeling that I had to have to work and especially in my relationship. How can I quit in a relationship?

I figured that I couldn't get rid of such an unpleasant and destructive habit. However, like everything else, practice makes it perfect. If you are training your mind with the right commitment, you don't have to overthink your life.

Writing this article also recalled many bitter memories of the way I used to be. I overanalyzed every little detail of what a friend said and how we were together when he expressed his feelings. It was so sick that I realized that this addiction would consume my life, if I didn't do anything about it, I would be the only one to be blamed.

Why Is Overthinking an Addiction?

A book by Dr. Sian Beilock Choke: What the secrets of the brain reveal when you have to explain this amazingly tiring event by quoting golf studies. They're a perfect analogy, as shocking as it is.

She says, when a professional golfer begins to think in the area, it is just a shy thought of missing the hole and losing the game. It's because our subconscious often paralyzes our body and paralyzes it anxiously, just a second or two. The fear of failure is typically the one to blame.

Overthinking is persistent paralysis of a golfer. As many empirical studies have shown, when we start losing control, it is a strategy that we use. Errors frighten us, confusion is overwhelming, and much can go wrong. So, we always think about it.

My sister cried clearly at a golf court, and I remembered because she could not play as well as I did. I wasn't a better player, don't get me wrong, but what helped me win the games came about. After all, I didn't care about it because I didn't overthink everything. I've been there for fun.

Addictive Behaviors

When you think about it, overthinking is no different from OCD. They ought to make life less unpredictable and give us a sense of control and trust. We only superintend our thoughts instead of establishing dominance over things.

In psychology, every conduct that is brought to bear by necessity, the behavior that thus turns to the most important thing in your life, but that leads to a conflict between short-term activity and long-term impacts–is defined as addictive.

It is often obsessed with overthinking when we have to control our lives. The problem is that what starts as a tactic that should calm us down usually leads us to lose control of our emotions. The vicious circle continues, with us in the middle.

Overthinking - Number One Relationship Killer

Two of my relationships ended badly because I'm overthinking, sad, but I'm sure some of you can relate. It's like I'm the only person to go crazy while everyone else enjoys their lives well; overthinking usually has consequences in my everyday life.

Like any other addiction, any time you have a problem, you don't think you can fix it or fear that you don't have the strength to overcome it. But is your relationship irresistible enough to kill? The experience says yes.

To overthink is a barricade between problem and solution; it disguises your fear of failure and makes you very cautious, depressingly motionless, and even more anxious.

Most notably, it's blocking you. You lose your self-confidence and esteem in your partner. All that works in partnerships is no longer there. The future is no longer about nourishing love and respect; it is nothing but a prediction of loss for an over-thinking person.

Low Self-Esteem – Root of Overthinking

You know what lies underneath your intense meditations, although it may not be the easiest thing to admit. The compulsive thought goes hand in hand with rattled self-confidence and happens when you feel inadequate. However, in case you need to learn how to stop thinking, self-analysis may be a good way to begin.

I was tricked once, and it was sufficient to make a large hole in my trust, my insecurity grew, and my confidence was no longer there.

When I looked back, I felt bad for my boyfriend. If he came home late or if he didn't call when he should, my mind was going out like an alarm clock, and the thoughts started to shed, and I fell back into the darkness. It took me a year to heal and trust again when my self-esteem was taken away.

It's not easy to work on low self-esteem, but I met my friend and now my husband, who knows me as I am. And one thing I want you to remember is that if you lack faith in yourself due to what happened to you in the past, trust them a little. Let them place you in front of the mirror and tell you how good you are, both inside and outside.

WAYS TO STOP RELATIONSHIP OVERTHINKING?

I'm not here to tell you that there's a magic to stop all these things now and forever, but I am here to share my tips on how to stop thinking in relationships.

Let us, therefore, be frank with you and move in the right direction with these suggestions below.

1. Iron Things out with Your Partner:

So, here's your first task; suggest a tête-au-tête as early as today. Talk things out with your partner, overthinking has made you a prisoner of mind, and your thoughts need to be expressed. Even if you two went through it before, now isn't the time to stop talking about things.

You know the processes of your partner by heart, so tailor what you have to say to how they respond. If you have been accused of exaggerating the problem in the past, be cool and constructive and ask them to do a little investigation. Understanding how addictive behavior functions will allow them to understand you better.

If it becomes painful and comes to a close, so be it. For a healthy relationship, you should never lack the ability to communicate your thoughts and emotions. As we know, silence is a lack of motion, but relationships must develop and change to survive.

Stay composed, be as descriptive as you can, and insist on expressing yourself. Your partner may feel confused and frightened, so be patient. Being in love means you are together in this; don't stop talking because you're also on the same page.

2. Stop Yourself The Moment You Find That You're Over-Analyzing The Actions Of Your Partner

A supportive partner is a sorely needed friend to fight negative thoughts, but only as long as you meet them halfway. Now that you have realized that your concerns were and remain unproductive, don't make it too complicated. Stressing how you deal with it will immediately drag you into it.

Rather, stop as soon as you catch your mind and rile up. Whether you are used to overanalyzing the expressions of your friends, dwelling on their Freudian mistakes, or obsessing about the ascent of a stranger that you constantly detect on it, note that your assumptions were wrong, and your thought was excessive.

3. Make Action On Your Insecurities (It's What Makes You An Over-thinker In First Place)

Improving your confidence is another subject, some of the things you can do as a point of departure. Silence your internal critic by acknowledging that no one is fine, and you are neither. Count every small victory, and show that you have earned the reward on your own. You can certainly appreciate it a lot, if it helps, write it down.

Be constructive, then! When you found that you overthought the actions of your partner because you were unsure of your looks, hit the gym! Perhaps your anger or insecurity is why you stress "how they say it;" learn how to shake it out. It takes some exercise, but you can nip your overthinking in the bud as long as you take action and be positive.

4. Always Have Some "Me Time" Every Day

You'll likely want to avoid those long, silent moments when all the noise in your head is overwhelming. This is not, though, when you should race alone. Have a "me" time every day, unplug the brain from the Television and telephone, and come into positive thinking.

You cannot fully tone down and rest your mind until you are left alone. Nonetheless, don't allow this overthinking to stop all of it. Since the lack of any diversion can cause your addictive behavior to intensify, your "me" time is great for regulation.

Try to rationalize; therefore, don't overthink it, but deduce if your partner does not respond to your calls. If everything's good, but you keep looking for at least one small thing to create a problem, just breathe deeply, close your eyes, and let meditation clear your brain.

5. Hang Out With Friends Who're Not Over-Thinkers

It is very important to talk to people who don't make things worse. Your logical friends probably are the last to tell you how to stop thinking in a relationship, but they can't help. In reality, their clear thinking is just what you need to resolve all those uncertainties.

We can and should become your everyday part of reality because they are so clear-sighted. The earlier you let your worries go, the more confusing your feelings are that nobody can understand you, the better you can resolve them and see what your problems are.

Don't discard the views of your friends, no matter how harsh or simplified they may appear. Rational people have a completely different world view, and the truth is always somewhere between them. Always be attentive to listen to what they have to say: their views that prove to be so much needed in time.

6. Ninety Percent Of What You Stress About Won't Happen, Always Enjoy Every Good Time

We already discussed how overthinking in a relationship almost always leads to a lack of spontaneity. Perhaps it happened to you before–you want to relax and enjoy the moment, but your feelings are all that you can think about. Awful, okay?

The fact is that most of the things you think about at that time are only fragments of your ruminant imagination. Around 90% of your worries will not be up to date, but your relationship will constantly be destroyed. Instead of thinking about how to stop in a relationship, try to be attentive and present at the moment.

And this is why it is so incredibly important to regain control of your mind. Love is not only about making plans and solving problems; it's more about building trust and allowing emotions to flood your thoughts than anything else. Do not allow those intimate moments to pass through you, but enjoy each second.

7. Keep Your Mind Busy With What Makes You A Great Person

Depression is similar to overthinking in some respects. If you examine your patterns more closely, you realize that over-analysis is nothing but a time delay mechanism; the longer you think of the problem, the more you postpone acting upon it.

Then, what this mechanism prevents you from seeing is that it won't be resolved if the problem does exist. Why not skip ruminations and act directly? However, it turns out that it will hurt less than spending hours endlessly acting out various scenarios.

Keep your mind busy with ideas instead. Work all the time on yourself and do things that will help you to become the person you want to be. Facing your challenges, you are less afraid of your constraints. Begin to work out, learn more, and think less about it.

8. Traveling with your partner at Least Once a Year

Research shows that holiday enhances ties and helps partners to look at each other in another way. It is entirely important since these fast-paced modern times suggest a speed that not all couples can bear. Holidays are a brilliant way to escape everything and finally find time to rekindle the romance.

At least once a year, travel together! When you encounter the world hand in hand, you can not only have a good time alone but also change your minds, reflecting on what is important. Traveling changes teaches patience and introduces serenity simply by showing you that there is a large world out there that is perhaps not so big in your everyday struggle.

9. Ask Your Partner What Kind Of Self-Improvement Can You Do To Preserve The Relationship

Your last task is simple; understand that you sometimes have to ask for everything you need to do. Your low self-confidence made you doubt the actions of your partner? Tell them what's happening! In case you have a good and stable relationship, their answer will be frank and helpful.

After all, there may be some things that bother you. Yet, you should never change who you are. It does take some compromise to be in a relationship. Talk to your partner about your reservations and see if you can resolve them and how.

And don't be overly sensitive! It is very important to allow your partner to speak, even though what they have to say is not so enjoyable for you to hear. They mean well, undoubtedly, so listen to them. It's much better than trying to sort out all the feelings yourself.

10. Be with That Person That Makes You Happy

Lastly, always keep in mind that symbiotic relationships are not very good. Who can make you happy? A strong couple is a partnership of two strong individuals, and if you're not a solid person, you can't be a strong partner. Never stop your personal growth–it can only be counterproductive for someone you love.

If you continue to think about your partner's unhappiness or not and why it usually means that you are not happy with yourself first and foremost, remember that you are that independent person who has it to improve and create, which is what your partner loves you so much.

11. Make Yourself Available And Stop Wandering

Relationships are challenging! We should be like that, so let nobody tell you otherwise. Give storytellers unconditional love and agree the true relationship requires understanding, trust, and respect. If you don't know how to stop your relationship overthinking, just ask your partner.

Above all, don't get wrapped in your head-express your feelings, express your views, articulate your fears, and share your doubts. Thinking overbuilds a wall of unproductive emotions while thinking about them is the simplest solution. Stay strong but articulate with your partner.

CHAPTER 10

OVERCOMING NEGATIVE THOUGHTS IN YOUR RELATIONSHIP

Negative thinking patterns make life less satisfactory when they keep you stuck in between what's wrong and what's right. Negative thinking often interferes with what you want. It makes you feel sad, depressed, and unhappy.

If the glass is half empty, it is almost difficult in each encounter to see the positive, potential, or silver linings and life lessons. In a partnership, it is extremely difficult for you or your partner to be content with this mindset. If your partner feels he or she can't please you and maximize your satisfaction. For example, he or she can feel less, weak, inadequate, etc. If you believe that your partner never does anything good enough, there may be relationships of friction, stress, and frustration. This dynamic, unfortunately, can easily become a vicious cycle of negativity.

You earn the energy you bring into the universe so that

when you dwell on the negative, you can see and get into your relationships. While unintentionally or consciously, you may have developed false beliefs to shield yourself from damage or disappointment, it is time to create a positive change to maintain a healthy, loving relationship. I understand that it may feel easier not to get your hopes on a new relationship (especially if you were previously heartbroken), but is it not one of your priorities to find someone who is amazing and thriving as a couple? If you have answered yes, this is an opportunity to turn your pessimistic lens into a more rational and positive attitude.

How To Overcome Negative Thinking

This is how:

1. ***Honestly assess your beliefs about yourself, relationship, world, and what you wish for in life.*** Do you believe like "Nothing works for me," "Men (or women) always hurt me" or "The world is a hideous place? If your words sound like some of the ones above, you think bad.

2. ***Take control of your negative ideas.*** Let us use the instance, "Nothing works for me," that feels

148

heavy, definitive, and permanent. Adjust this idea internally to create room to figure out stuff for you and to appreciate all that has done well for you. Talk about your memories and note that life has gone well for you many times. Try various positive thoughts and see what feels right. For example, "I am open to meaningful interaction in my life and love." "I am thankful for "or "I can manage my life."

3. ***Rewire your brain.*** Recognize and transform a negative thought or belief into one of the most positive thoughts you have developed. This is an unbelievably important change in your mind. So it takes time, energy, and persistence to get the idea you want in a safer, new way. However, once you constantly correct it, you will see that your negative thoughts dissipate, and healthier ones arise. This is how you take down the negative lens and look at the world more honestly and with more hope.

A few other tips to make your dating and relationship life more satisfying as you change your mind to achieve the love you wish for...

- **_Always remember that taking care of your expectations is important to your relationship's success._** Discrepancies and conflicts are inevitable in the world of relations, so remember that it's natural and all right. The most important thing is how you and your partner manage and develop in difficult times.

- **_Remember, your partner is also a person._** Not all your partner does is "right" or "good," but you resist the urge to change your critical lens when you are frustrated. Communicate on your desires, and don't try to generalize the entire relationship for a moment when you feel hurt.

- **_Consider the partner deliberately in a positive light._** Thank him/her for the little things and compassion that your partner shows. Say, thank you. It perpetuates a cycle of optimistic and caring relationships.

- **_Don't take things personally._** There will be poor dates, difficult conversations, and times that can be frustrating at the time. Do not add these experiences to your negative pile–take life lessons instead imagine yourself moving towards your goals. Engage yourself to be happy on your journey to marriage.

PREVENTING TOXIC THOUGHTS FROM AFFECTING YOUR RELATIONSHIP

There are great numbers of things that can ruin an entirely good relationship. Cheating and incompatibility, for example, are two major issues. According to scientists, there is one thing that can be more than anything else that ruins a relationship.

The biggest killer of the relationship can be negative thoughts, "says Bustle, licensed psychologist Nicole Issa, Psy. D. "There is a very close feedback link between the emotions, feelings, and actions. Having negative thoughts will take you down the rabbit hole." It is important to know from Dr. Issa that your thinking habits will contribute to important problems with your relationships. For example, early childhood encounters with your parents can make you feel unworthy of love. That is why you may get into all relationships believing that at some stage, your partner is about to abandon you, and you may be afraid to speak up.

"The truth is that we are making our reality," Joann Cohen, matchmaker and dating coach, says to Bustle. "If we believe we have a good relationship, we work through things that believe that things are always ok. But when you come to relationships with a negative thought, you always expect the worst not only for your partner but also for the outcome of your relationship." You need to find ways to make them positive to prevent negative thoughts. Listed below are some things you can do to stop toxic ideas, according to experts, sabotaging your relationship.

1. Think about the first time you have fallen in love with your Spouse

When you pass a rough patch, it is easy to let that cloud judge you. Talk about the "real" feelings of your partner when you start invading your mind, the first time you fell in love with them, and talk about how you felt. "Shutting your eyes and seeing the bright eye person with whom you fell in love will make things look much more positive and doable," says Cohen. At times, we need only a little reminder of the good times to resolve the poor.

2. Letting Go of the Past

Honestly, letting go of the past is easier said than done. To be fair, "We all have a piece of our history with us to' shield' us against getting hurt again," says Cohen. "And if you continue to bring your old relations harm to your new relationship, then you sabotage and create the truth that things just do not or will not work." Then, try to separate your past from your present, to prevent your past from creating toxic thoughts. No matter how much they look, speak, or behave the same, your ex isn't your current partner. If you can separate your previous relationship from your new one, being more involved is much easier for you.

3. Find other ways to channel your energy

Toxic thinking will cause you to do unreasonable, relationship-sabotage stuff like hack into your partner's phone or sabotage. To counter this phenomenon, Dr. Issa says that he knows what your thoughts are doing. For instance, why do you feel you need to just "check-in" your partner 20 times in a row? You would also want some affirmation or confirmation that your partner cares. "Once you know that you can do (these) stuff, take some time to practice those skills to help you to count to ten and relax," she says. Find ways to reduce the intense feelings you have so that you will not act in ways that you will regret later.

4. Stop Assuming That you Know What Your Partner Is Thinking

Negative thoughts are more often than not based on perceptions that do not always exist. "If we put our negative feelings on somebody else or place them on another person, the anger of the other person is what you are reading," Cohen says. The important thing here is never to presume. Do not jump to conclusions. Don't cook it yourself if you can't help it. Get to the edge and chat with your friend. "Try or ask for clarification, take the words on face value," she says. "You never believe you know how they feel."

5. Have That One Person You go to, to Vent Your anger

If you are mad about your partner, it's not uncommon to put all your problems to anyone who's listening. But, according to Cohen, "When you do that, you create a gap between your meaningful other person and your world, creating more negativity than you know." If you have to lower yourself down, choose one person, and stay with them. "Saying to everyone is not helpful to your ugly business and will only encourage more negative feelings," she says.

6. Create A List Of Your Toxic Thoughts And Come Up With Positive Ones

Preventing toxic thoughts from destruction takes some self-reflection with constructive alternatives. However, one best thing to do while reflecting is to physically write out all the typical ideas that lead to struggles or even divisions. Take it a step further and write hard proof for or against any thought. After that, come up with a more concise and adaptive alternative thinking. For instance, if you think your partner is no longer interested in you because they didn't reply to your text, please list all other things they could do. "Think about other occasions they have taken a while to answer or to show that they're still involved," says Dr.Issa. "Here the alternative thought may be as simple as' just as I haven't heard of them yet it doesn't mean they don't care.'" Then, the more detailed you are, the more effective it will be.

7. Take Breaking-up Totally Off The Table

Whatever the toxic thoughts are, usually, they are from the same location — fear. In particular, the fear that your partner will leave. "I use the analogy, you' burn the ship' when you comment," Cohen says. "There is no way to get out of the island when you burn the ship, so work together to survive." If there is no solution, you start seeing what is good in a situation. When you take the chance to break the equation (that is "burning the ship"), you can support your relationship from a place of love and not fear. If your words and actions come from a place of affection, it's much easier for you to remain positive.

Thinking is only a thought at the end of the day. It's not necessarily the truth. If you don't let your relationship consume you, it will improve your relationship.

CHAPTER 11

OVERCOMING FEAR OF ABANDONMENT IN A RELATIONSHIP

ear of abandonment is the overriding fear that people near you will leave. Everyone can develop a fear of giving up. It can be deeply rooted in your traumatic experience as a child or in adult depression.

When you fear failure, maintaining healthy relationships can be almost impossible. The paralyzing fear will bring you down to the wall to avoid being harmed. Or you may be sabotaging partnerships unintentionally.

The first step to overcoming anxiety is to understand why you feel like that. You can address your fears on your own or through therapy. However, fear of abandonment may also be part of a personality disorder requiring treatment.

Continue to read and discuss the origins and long-term effects of the fear of abandonment.

Different Types of Fear of Abandonment

You may fear that someone you love will physically leave and not come back—examples of abandonment fear. You might be afraid someone will give up your emotional needs. You can either maintain yourself in ties with a parent, partner, or friend.

Fear of Emotional Abandonment

This can somewhat be less noticeable, but it is no less painful. Emotional needs exist for us all. In case these conditions are not met, you may feel unrecognized, unloved, and disconnected. You may feel very much alone, even if you are in a relationship with a physically present person.

If you have undergone emotional renunciation in the past, especially as a child, you may be constantly afraid that it will happen again.

Fear of Abandonment In Children

It is normal for babies and children to experience a period of separation fear.

You may scream, yell, or refuse to let go if a parent or caregiver is leaving. At this stage, children have difficulty understanding when or if the person will return.

As they begin to understand that they come back, they resolve their terror. This happens to most children by their 3rd birthday.

Abandonment Anxiety In relationships

You can be afraid of allowing yourself to be insecure in a relationship. You may have problems with confidence and worry about your relationship too much. That can make your partner suspicious.

Over time, the anxieties will cause the other person to retreat and keep the cycle going.

Symptoms of The Fears Of Abandonment

When you fear abandonment, you can likely identify some of these symptoms and signs:

- Too sensitive to criticism

- Trouble trusting in others

- Difficulty making friends unless you are sure you want them

- Take extreme measures to prevent rejections or separation

- A pattern of unhealthy relationships

- Staying in a relationship even at the point that it is not healthy for you

- Blaming yourself when things don't work

- Trouble committing into a relationship

- Working too hard to please people

- Getting attached to people quickly and moving on quickly

Causes of Abandonment

Abandonment problems in relationships may be due to having been emotionally or physically abandoned in the past.

For example:

- As an infant, a parent or caregiver may be dead or abandoned.

- Parental negligence may have been felt.

- Your colleagues might have rejected you.

- You have been through a loved one's chronic illness.

- A romantic partner may have suddenly left you or acted untruthfully.

These events can lead to a fear of abandonment.

Avoidant Personality Disorder

An avoidant personality disorder is a personality disorder that may include anxiety and a socially depressed or deficient sense of abandonment.

- Nervousness

- Poor self-esteem

- Extreme fear of negative judgment

- Disqualification in social settings

- Avoidance of group and self-imposed social isolation

Borderline Personality Disorder

A borderline personality disorder is another personality disorder, where intense fear of rejection will play a part.

- Unstable relationships

- Distorted self-images

- Extreme impulsiveness

- Mood swings and anger

- Difficulty being alone

Many people who have limited personality disorders say they have been sexually or physically abused as children. Many grew up amid violent strife or communities with the same illness.

Separation Anxiety Disorder

If a child does not resolve anxiety about separation, and it interferes with daily work, a separation anxiety disorder can occur.

The signs and symptoms include the following:

- Panic attacks

- Depression with the thought of the separation of people we love

- Persistent refusal to leave home without a loved one or

to be alone

- Hallucinations with separation of loved ones

- Physics problems such as stomach pain or headache, when separated from loved ones, Teens, and adults that experience anxiety about separation.

Long-Term Effects of Fear of Abandonment

The long term effects of the fear of giving up may include:

- Challenging connections with friends and romantic partners

- Poor self-esteem

- Issues with self-confidence

- Mood swings

- Codependence

- Depression

- Fear of intimacy

- Panic problems

Examples of the Fear of Abandonment

Listed below are a few examples of what the fear of giving up may look like:

Longer-term effects of fear of abandonment You may think, "No connection, no drop."

- You are obsessively worried about your perceived flaws and what others might think about you.

- You are the most pleasant people. You don't want to take any opportunity that someone doesn't like you to stay there.

- You are crushed when someone criticizes you a little or gets upset in any way.

- When you feel slighted, you overreact

- You feel insufficient and unattractive.

- You split with a romantic partner so that they can't break up.

- Even if the other person asks for space, you are clingy.

- You are often jealous, suspicious of your partner,

or critical of him.

Fear of abandonment is not a diagnosed mental health disorder, but it can be certainly detected and discussed. Diagnosing fear of abandonment Fear of rejection may also be part of a diagnosable personality or other condition to be treated.

Recovery Problems

Once you know that you fear loss, you can do some things to start recovery. Remove some slackness and stop the harsh judgment on yourself. Mind all the positive qualities that make you a good partner and mate.

Speak to the other person and how it came to be about the fear of abandonment. But be aware of what you deserve from others. Explain where you come from, but don't make something to fix your fear of abandonment. Don't expect more than is fair from them.

Work to maintain friendships and build a support network. Strong friendships will strengthen your sense of belonging and self-worth.

If this is not practical, consider talking to a qualified therapist. You will benefit from individual advice.

How to Assist Someone With Abandonment Problems

Some strategies for trying if someone you know has to deal with the fear of abandonment:

- Begin the conversation. Encourage them to speak, but don't press.

- Understand that fear is real for you, whether it makes sense or not.

- Make sure you're not going to abandon them.

- Ask what you can do to assist.

Suggest treatment, but don't push it. If you want to start, offer your help in finding a professional therapist.

See your healthcare provider for guidance if you have attempted but are unable to manage your fear of self-abandonment or if you have signs of panic disorder, anxiety disorder, or depression.

You should continue a full check-up with your primary care physician. You can then consult a doctor to diagnose and treat the illness.

Personality disorders can lead to depression, substance

use, and social isolation without treatment.

Fear of abandonment will affect your relationships negatively. But you can do things to minimize these fears.

If the fear of dropping out is part of a broader personality disorder, drugs and psychotherapy can be successfully treated.

CHAPTER 12
ADVICE FOR COUPLES

Communications are pragmatic and need a variety, of course, corrections to optimize their ability. You can strengthen the condition by experiencing the effect of anger problems, poor communication, or an inability to compromise. Developing open and honest communication tools, learning to strike a compromise and committing to change would make you happy.

Improving Communication

- *Plan what you would like to say:* Write down your concerns to let your spouse know. It helps to identify other attitudes, emotions, and remedies. Include a possible solution if you think there is a problem.

* Write your thoughts down. It will be good to get everything out on paper. Writing your thoughts is therapeutic and will help organize your emotions in a way that promotes stress reduction.

* Always be prepared to combat that urge to be negative, and also in a situation you want to talk to someone who might overwhelm you with their negativity.

* Always practice and say your concerns out loud. Don't think that you're fine. If you think about someone who can overwhelm you with his anger, being prepared is a good way to fight the temptation to be pessimistic as well.

-        ***Choose a good time to speak:*** Stop talks early in the morning when you or your partner may be rude, and try not to talk when you come home from work. Relax and relax before you get there. When you felt the brunt of his anger, you undoubtedly know the time to reach a positive outcome.

• Public talk could be helpful. The person is less likely to be upset because of fear of embarrassment.

• To set the stage for positive interactions, coordinate as many positive things as possible. Maybe you can go somewhere you both enjoy or stay at home and have a great dinner.

-    ***Keep a positive attitude while chatting.*** Express
your optimism about collaborating to find a solution. This
is your opportunity to change your relationship. It's time
to talk and to be heard. Don't let your spouse stop you
from having a good conversation that resolves problems.
You are on the task of being heard so that you focus on
what is important to create change for the better.

- To take a positive approach to this subject by saying
  something like, "I very much appreciate what you
  do for me, and I want to be glad about it. I believe
  that, based on some things you say, you are not
  pleased with me. "That will start things off.

- If the first response is negative, try to stop him
  saying, "I want to talk about it calmly because I'm
  worried about it; if we need something to improve,
  then we need to listen to each other."

- If he can not respond without getting aggressive or
  upset, just say, "Maybe we can talk later on." If he
  is absolute in his way, you have a more serious
  problem in your hands. Don't be detrimental to
  yourself. Take as much as you can to a safe place.

- He should reply with an open ear and demonstrate his genuine concern to you. This is your opportunity to let him know how misunderstood you are. Don't be afraid to tell him your feelings hurt, and your friendship and future scare you.

- Continue to tell him you love him and show your support for what he has to say.

- ***Find out what's happening***. If you know you have done nothing that would be a negative response for your spouse, however, it's time to roll-up your sleeves and work. This is the ideal opportunity to practice your problem-solving capabilities.

* If a person still worries or criticizes certain things in life, this may be because of something he has encountered earlier in life. There could be an incident or a tragic event in the life of a person that makes him do so.

* You can find that he is very unhappy about his work or an insignificant issue with which you have nothing to do. When he thinks his life is bad for these things, he might take it on you.

* He might be resentful that you are not perfect. You

need to remind him that you're not perfect; you haven't always been when you met.

* Insecurities about the performance of work, financial independence, and physical performance can all lead to a person's constant complaint and negative performance.

* He might think the world is against him and he may believe you are part of it. You have to be isolated to convince him that you are on his side.

-        ***Be honest.*** Lead by example and tell your truth. This doesn't imply that you have to be brutally honest and injure the feelings of the individual. Use your words carefully and note that you are trying to solve issues that will strengthen your relationship with your communication.

-        ***Be polite and, in exchange, ask for it.*** Respect has been won. When you behave respectfully, it will set the stage for appreciation. If you feel you are not valued, tell the person, "I want us to be mutually respectful. I'm happy to do that, are you?

-        ***Be open.*** To be weak takes courage. It is important to open your heart to the possibility of change.

You might be afraid to get hurt, but that's a chance. Once you have the opportunity to be free, it will be simpler.

1. Combating the Inability To Compromise

- **Set The Stage For A Resolution.** Lead by example and act as a mediator for yourself. You would like to be positive about the situation. Be patient and concentrate so that she knows you're serious and that you can solve the problem.

* *Be diplomatic.* A keen sense of fairness will help you do your work.

* *Be heard and listen.* As we all know, it is common knowledge that you cannot listen and speak simultaneously. You must know what she has to say, and you must believe that you have heard. Tell her if you don't feel what you've heard.

* *Do not interrupt.* Show your appreciation by not interrupting the flow. You tell her something like, if she interrupts, "I'm not going to interrupt you when you talk, because I want to hear what you have to say. Please allow me to speak without interruption so that you would know exactly what I'm trying to tell.

- **Ask "What You Want.** Know what you want and express it. She must know how you feel when she criticizes your stuff. Consider these things in advance so that you can communicate your needs and desires. Preparing will help you stay on the job if you decide to add negative feedback.

* ***Do not jeopardize your beliefs.*** Be transparent that you are not willing to compromise your principles. Specify what you see as deal-breakers. Ask her if she constantly mocks your grandmother behind you, which erodes your family's dignity.

* Always bind the needs together and want to support the relationship. Confirm that everything you want is to be fulfilled and happy with her.

- **Always Ask Her What She Wants.** This will enable her to clarify her requests, expectations, and wishes. It is important to hear what she has to say so that she feels understood.

* Take notes and if she tells you why you do that, tell her that you don't want to miss something She says. Take notes.

* Read her your notes and ask if it's all right. Add anything you've missed or something she wants to add.

* If she says anything that she wants and you know that you can't agree, just say, "I can't. To me, that's not fair. Maybe we could take some time to consider other options and find a compromise.

-       **Avoid Negativity**. People with chronic anxiety issues give a pessimistic twist to any case. Do not allow yourself to be affected by negative and critical thinking of your partner.

* When she continues to be pessimistic, tell her, "I try to concentrate on the positive so we can solve the problem. It's quick to be evil. It's difficult to be constructive, but that's what I'll do.

-       **Solicit a Commitment of Change.** You will also completely embrace the concept of reconciliation. You must decide to try to make a change, at least. That may be your point of departure, and you can build from there. The goal is to participate fully in the process, but you may need to begin with small steps.

* Check the products on both lists. Let her know that

if she also agrees to make the changes, you understand?

* Such things as "I am willing to commit to you, and this agreement is acceptable.

* Trust her, to make things better for you both and your future together.

2. Imperfection Adjustment

-        *Be careful.* For some people, change isn't easy. Your partner is facing a difficult challenge, particularly if he has not been aware of what triggers his behavior. The key to success is discipline. Convince yourself that this is a very difficult time, but it is temporary.

* If you continue to focus on your goals, things will improve.

* Don't give up if things aren't going right. Discuss the issue and decide if necessary to make changes.

-        ***Appreciate one another.*** When you're satisfied with what's going on, tell your wife. If you see that he is pessimistic, and then he corrects himself, he acknowledges this as an achievement. They must know that they're doing a good job. It will allow you both to stay inspired.

176

- ***Laugh.*** If you can both find a way to laugh at the situation, it can cure you both. As I have realized over time, the shortest distance between two people is a laugh. If you chuckle, it is almost hard to be angry. Say it. Do it.

- ***Be coachable.*** A little coaching is required for everyone. Don't blame your wife or yourself for fault. Concentrate instead on the efforts you both make to be better people. A little step in the right direction is still a step.

- ***Let it go.*** It is important to keep things in perspective, whether your situation is more difficult or if you deal with a spouse who does not accept your request to take out the trash. Nobody likes to feel small, inferior, or overlooked by a partner or by anybody. You should find that once you feel listened to and appreciated, you will express your feelings of frustration and relief. You can let go of it.

  - If you are struggling to let something go and continues to eat at you, you probably have to eat more of the problem. This can include more conversation with your partner or taking a walk to sort out your feelings physically.

- If someone says "let it go," it can be upsetting if you haven't achieved a degree of resolve in this matter. Endeavor to take a deep breath and say, "I'm working on letting go, but I'm not yet there.

- When you feel like you're happy, you see some things worth getting upset, and some don't.

-        ***Renew your Commitment.*** For various reasons, many people decide to renew their wedding or commitment vows. This can be a great opportunity to show each other in the ceremony that you have not lost interest in your relationship and are still in love.

It can lead to a stronger desire for commitment during tough times together.

Your wife may realize the pain it has caused and may feel guilty. Maybe he's going to show you he's sorry for what he's done. Let him.

3. Search Help

-        ***Be autonomous.*** Happiness is a job inside, and you must create it. You always know what makes you happy, so take part in activities that create a reservoir of positive feelings outside of your relationship. If you are packed with good vibes, it's easier to face negative and challenging men. A happy friendship, you will always change.

-        ***Find a positive energy source.*** It can be very tiring and difficult to deal with people who are always pessimistic. Changing takes time so that you need support and encouragement to fight. Find a friend you trust and who can be an inspiring source.

* Note that negative people are draining us from our ability to replace it. Camp, dance, yoga, and golf are just a few ways to recharge the batteries.

-        ***Avoid people with detrimental characteristics:*** Keep away from negative and unsupportive friends and other family members. It's best left to these men. Don't let them affect your wife's relationship.

* If it were easy to be happy, everyone would do it. In this world, there is a great deal of discontent, and many people like to say it without permission. You don't have to hear it.

- ***Consult with a professional.*** When you find that the problem cannot be handled, there are qualified psychologists, therapists, and mediators who can assist. You are human, and sometimes you get to the end of your rope and need help. Although a breakup or divorce will be complicated, it may be the only solution to your problem.

* Finally, a temporary separation could save your relationship. This may give you the right distance, which helps you to save time to determine the relationship.

* In your local area, psychologists and psychiatrists can be found through the U.S. and the American Psychiatric Association.

* A mediator is a party who tries to make a settlement easier for both sides.

CONCLUSION

Anxiety relationship is a type of anxiety that can be difficult for health care professionals to diagnose and treat. Many of the symptoms identified by people with anxiety are also typical in other types of anxiety.

Relationship anxiety signs may include self-silence and constant reassurance. People with relationship anxiety may also want their partner's acceptance and fear rejection. These symptoms can harm the relationship over time.

Couples psychoeducation and therapy are different approaches that doctors offer people with anxiety about relationships. Some physicians may need to prescribe drugs in extreme cases.

www.ingramcontent.com/pod-product-compliance
Lightning Source LLC
Chambersburg PA
CBHW031111250726
48655CB00004B/1666